ECONOMICS

D.R. OLSON

Preface

In this book I present principles of economics.

D.R. Olson
17 September 2020

Contents

II Coercion

III Examples

PART I

The Free Market

1

Axioms and Definitions

1.1 Human Action

Sound economic theory derives logically from incontrovertible axioms of human action. First, human beings act as individuals. Societies and groups have no independent existence apart from their members. Institutions do not and cannot act; rather, individuals that constitute institutions act.

Second, human beings act purposefully to achieve certain ends. A person will not act if all of his needs and wants are satisfied.

Third, human beings act to achieve ends using scarce means. A person can allocate his time and resources toward only a finite number of ends. He must leave some of his needs or wants unsatisfied.

Fourth, human beings act according to unique scales of values that they place on ends. Each person evaluates ends subjectively (but unquantifiably and immeasurably) and ranks them in order of preference. No two people will place the same values on all ends.

1.2 Goods

Human beings use *goods* to achieve ends. Every exchangeable good is either tangible (a *material*) or intangible (a *service*). People derive the values that they place on units of goods from the values that they place on the ends that those units can satisfy; hence the values that they place on units of goods may change as the values that they place on ends change. As a person procures more units of a good, he can better satisfy the end toward which he would apply that good and his need or desire for still another unit will be less acute. Thus he will place less value on the nth unit of a good that he possesses than on each of the first $n - 1$ units.

Before someone can consume a good, someone must produce it. People produce tangible goods by mixing their *labor* with *ingredients* by means of *plant*. Plant (buildings, tools, equipment, machinery, and like materials) are tangible goods themselves that people have produced. Ingredients (the components of a tangible good) can be either tangible goods that people have produced or raw materials (*natural resources*) that exist naturally in the universe. Labor (work) is an intangible good. Resolved into its basic elements, every good is a mixture of labor and natural resources.

Products that differ in substance, size, shape, location, condition, grade, or any other quality meaningful to traders in the market are different goods. Generally, the number of units in existence of a particular material will exceed one only when all of those units are unused, produced in mass, and sold in the same location, while the number of units in existence of a particular service will exceed one only when those units are provided by the same person in the same location under the same conditions.

1.3 Voluntary Exchange

Different people place different values on goods. Two people will trade units of goods voluntarily if and only if each of them places a higher value on the unit that the other person possesses than on the unit that he himself possesses. Hence voluntary exchange of goods brings benefit to both parties involved.

Social (as opposed to *anti-social*) action is voluntary interaction with others in a society. A *society* is a group of people who trade with each other, where each person in the group engages in commerce with at least one other person in the group. The members of a society will find more goods that better satisfy their needs and wants when they engage in greater exchange and greater production of a greater variety of goods.

1.4 Money

In a barter system, if a person owns units of good X and wishes to trade them for units of good Y, then he must either find an owner of units of Y who is willing to trade them for units of X, or he must find an owner of units of Y who is willing to trade them for units of good Z_n and then find owners of units of goods $Z_1, Z_2, Z_3, \ldots, Z_n$ with whom he can trade X for Z_1, then Z_1 for Z_2, then Z_2 for Z_3, $\ldots$, then Z_{n-1} for Z_n.

Money is a commodity that the members of a society accept as a medium of exchange. People trade goods indirectly through money (by first trading units of goods that they own for units of money and then trading units of money for units of goods that they want) because they cannot easily find parties with whom they can trade goods directly. Without a standard money to facilitate exchange, people must live primitively.

A monetary material should be scarce so that the money does not lose its value rapidly, divisible so that people can set prices of goods in terms of a small amount (the unit) of the money, portable so that people can carry the money to a point of sale, durable so that the money does not wear out quickly, and fungible so that any two units of the money will have the same size and quality. Different commodities have served as monetary material at different places and times in history, but gold and silver satisfy the qualities above best. Any money made of paper will lack scarcity because its producer can print it cheaply.

1.5 Purchases and Sales

Using money, people buy materials and services that they want or need and sell materials and services that they own or render. Most people sell their services more often than they sell their materials. People who frequently sell their materials usually come to own (either through production or through purchase for resale) large quantities of them. Such sellers include farmers, miners, merchants, and industrialists.

People want lower prices on goods when they buy them and higher prices on goods when they sell them. At any given time, the interval of prices at which a person would buy a unit of a good that he wants will have some upper limit and the interval of prices at which he would sell a unit of a good that he owns will have some lower limit.

1.6 Production and Consumption

People produce and sell goods primarily to obtain money with which to buy and consume other goods. When a person produces and sells more units of a good, he can afford to buy and consume more units of other goods. But at the same time, he will enable other members of society to consume more units of the good that he has produced. Though consumption can lag production considerably, the rate of production of a good will ultimately affect the rate of consumption of the good; greater production will enable greater consumption and less production will necessitate less consumption. The total amount of goods that the members of society consume can never exceed the total amount of goods that they produce.

1.7 Measures of Business

If a person produces and sells units of a good, then his:

- *revenues* are his receipts from sales;
- *expenses* are his costs of production;
- *profit* is his revenues less his expenses (if revenues exceed expenses);
- *loss* is his expenses less his revenues (if expenses exceed revenues);
- *capital* is the property (e.g., cash, land, plant) that he has accumulated in his business.

2

Prices

2.1 Supply and Demand

Different people place different values on goods that they own or wish to own (see section 1.3). The *demand* for a good at a certain price is the number of units of the good that people would buy at that price. The *supply* of a good at a certain price is the number of units of the good that their owners would sell at that price. Since potential buyers of a good normally enter the marketplace at scattered hours throughout a day, levels of demand and supply customarily reflect quantities desired and offered over periods of time rather than at instants in time. A *surplus* of a good will exist at prices where supply exceeds demand and a *shortage* of a good will exist at prices where demand exceeds supply.

Both the demand for a good and the supply of a good will assume exactly one value at each price over a given period of time. Hence we can indicate correlations between prices and levels of demand and supply by means of functions. We will use the letters d and s to represent the functions that perform these correlations so that $d(p)$ will equal the demand for a good and $s(p)$ will equal the supply of a good at the price p. A given function d or s can pertain to only a single good on a single period of time because we cannot combine meaningfully quantities of two disparate goods and because levels of demand and supply at various prices may differ over different periods of time. The graphs of d and s will be loci of isolated points in most cases because quantities usually assume values precise to the nearest unit of measure and prices usually assume values no more precise than a hundredth of the unit of money; however, we will depict d and s as step functions or continuous monotonic functions in most figures within this treatise (such as Figure 1) for simplicity.

Over a given period of time, the demand for a good at a lower price will be greater than or equal to the demand for the good at a higher price but the supply of a good at a lower price will be less than or equal to the supply of the good at a higher price (algebraically, if $p_1 < p_2$ then $d(p_1) \geq d(p_2)$ and $s(p_1) \leq s(p_2)$) because a low price will encourage buying and discourage selling while a high price will discourage buying and encourage selling. Hence a particle that traces a graph of demand from left to right will tend to descend, while a particle that traces a graph of supply from left to right will tend to ascend.

Points on a graph of supply will often align horizontally. If a producer must sell all n units of a good he holds in stock, then he must prefer any amount of money over any unit of the good. The formula $s(p) = n$ for $p \geq 0$ will then define the function s that returns the supply of the good. Formulas of this form pertain most obviously to perishable goods that lose value rapidly, but not exclusively to them. A person who produces multiple units of a nonperishable good may also hold them in low value subjectively because he will have no use for them himself and would rather sell them cheaply than incur expenses indefinitely for their storage and maintenance.

2.2 Settlement of Prices

A producer will usually wish to sell all units of his good within a certain period of time (avoiding a surplus) and at the highest price possible (avoiding a shortage). To meet both of these objectives, he must adjust the price of his good downward from values at which a surplus exists (that is, from p at which $s(p) > d(p)$) and upward from values at which a shortage exists (that is, from p at which $s(p) < d(p)$) until it reaches a state of equilibrium at a value where supply equals demand. The price will remain in equilibrium at that value as long as levels of supply and demand do not change from one period of time to the next and the producer maintains the same objectives with a single price for all buyers on a given period.

Since the value p_e at which the price of a good would reach equilibrium will normally be the solution to the equation $s(p) = d(p)$, the quantity q_e of the good that buyers and sellers would exchange at that price will equal both $s(p_e)$ and $d(p_e)$. Furthermore, the graphs of the equations $q = s(p)$ and $q = d(p)$ will intersect at the point with coordinates (p_e, q_e), assuming we draw those graphs in a two-dimensional plane with price p (the independent variable) on the horizontal axis and quantity q (the dependent variable) on the vertical axis. If the equation $s(p) = d(p)$ has more than one solution, then the graphs of supply and demand will intersect in more than one point and the price of the good would reach equilibrium at all values within some interval. If the equation $s(p) = d(p)$ has no solution, then the graphs of s and d will not intersect and the price of the good would not reach equilibrium at any value. In this case the price may temporarily settle at a point where either the function $d - s$ or the function $s - d$ attains its least positive value, but a shortage or a surplus of the good will develop inevitably.

The values at which the prices of different goods reach equilibrium will usually differ because schedules of supply and demand for different goods will differ, but schedules of supply and demand will determine for every good (both materials and services) the value at which its price reaches equilibrium. Though we often call a service *labor*, the price of a service a *wage* or a *salary*, the seller of a service a *worker* or *employee*, and the buyer of a service a *hirer* or *employer*, the existence of such terminology peculiar to services does not make our analysis less pertinent to them than to materials.

2.3 Effects of Changes in Supply or Demand on Prices

As levels of demand and supply change, the value at which the price of a good reaches equilibrium may also change. If the demand for a good rises (but the supply remains the same) or the supply of a good falls (but the demand remains the same) at a price that had reached equilibrium, then a shortage of the good will develop at that price and supply will now equal demand at a higher price (see Figures 1 and 2). On the other hand, if the demand for a good falls (but the supply remains the same) or the supply of a good rises (but the demand remains the same) at a price that had reached equilibrium, then a surplus of the good will develop at that price and supply will now equal demand at a lower price (see Figures 3 and 4).

We can summarize these principles succinctly with algebraic statements. Let d_1 and d_2 represent the functions that return the demand for a good, s_1 and s_2 represent the functions that return the supply of the good, and p_{e_1} and p_{e_2} represent the values at which the price of the good would reach equilibrium on two periods of time. Then:

- if $d_1(p_{e_1}) \leq d_2(p_{e_1})$ and $s_1(p_{e_1}) = s_2(p_{e_1})$, then $p_{e_1} \leq p_{e_2}$
- if $s_1(p_{e_1}) \geq s_2(p_{e_1})$ and $d_1(p_{e_1}) = d_2(p_{e_1})$, then $p_{e_1} \leq p_{e_2}$
- if $d_1(p_{e_1}) \geq d_2(p_{e_1})$ and $s_1(p_{e_1}) = s_2(p_{e_1})$, then $p_{e_1} \geq p_{e_2}$
- if $s_1(p_{e_1}) \leq s_2(p_{e_1})$ and $d_1(p_{e_1}) = d_2(p_{e_1})$, then $p_{e_1} \geq p_{e_2}$

We can expand these principles in a natural way if the price of the good would reach equilibrium at all values in the intervals I_{e_1} and I_{e_2} instead of at the points p_{e_1} and p_{e_2} only; we merely adjust our conclusions to state that the bounds of I_{e_1} will be less than or equal to the bounds of I_{e_2} in the first and second cases, but greater than or equal to the bounds of I_{e_2} in the third and fourth cases.

The demand for a good at any given price will generally be greater over a longer period of time than over a shorter period of time, so the value at which the price of a good would reach equilibrium will generally be higher over a longer period of time than over a shorter period of time if levels of supply of the good are the same over both periods. In fact, the price of a good in fixed supply will reach equilibrium at any arbitrarily high value on some sufficiently long period of time provided its producer can sell at least one unit of the good at that price regularly.

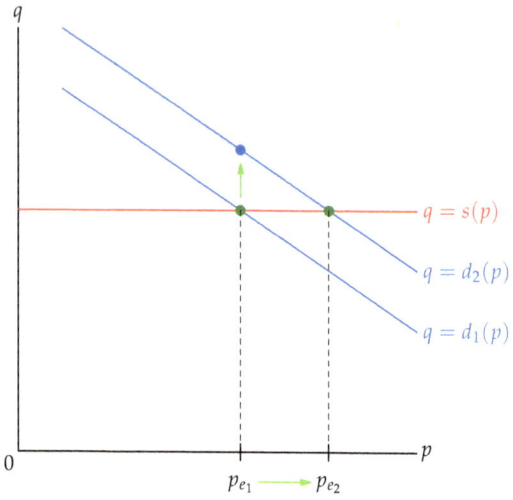

Figure 1: Increase in Demand

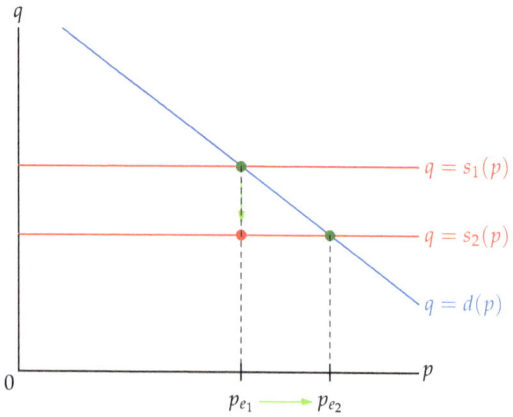

Figure 2: Decrease in Supply

14

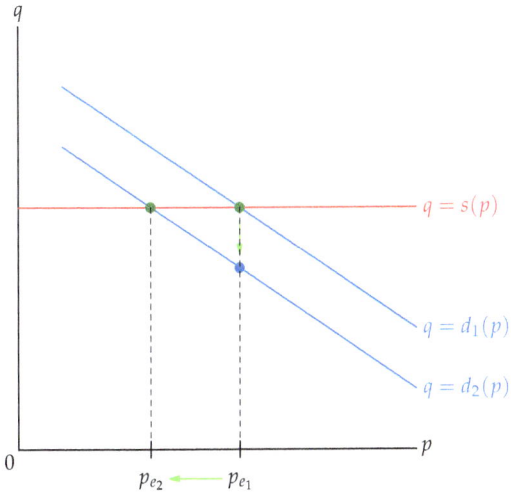

Figure 3: Decrease in Demand

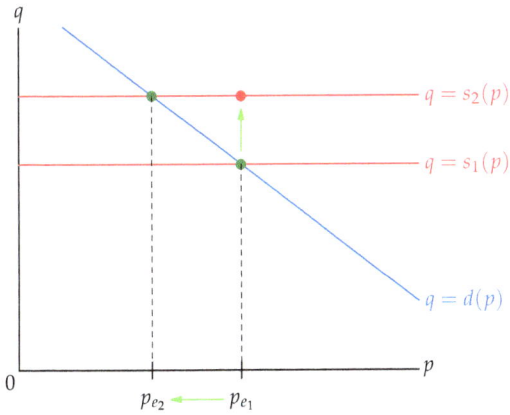

Figure 4: Increase in Supply

15

3

Changes in Supply and Demand

3.1 Direct Causes of Changes in the Demand for Goods

Levels of demand for a good change when the willingness and ability of people to buy units of it change. These levels need not rise or fall uniformly across all prices. In fact, the demand at one price may rise while the demand at another price falls.

The willingness of a person to buy a unit of a good reflects the value that he places on the unit relative to the values that he places on units of money in consideration of the other ways in which he might dispense that money. When he places greater relative value on the unit, the demand for the good will rise on some prices; when he places less relative value on the unit, the demand for the good will fall on some prices. These values can change as his needs or wants change, as he learns about other items available in the market, or as the quality of the good improves or deteriorates (though modifications to a good will transform it into a different good altogether).

The ability of a person to buy a unit of a good reflects the amount of money that he possesses. When the amount of money that he possesses increases, he can afford to pay more money for the unit so the demand for the good will rise on some prices. When the amount of money that he possesses decreases, the demand for the good will fall on some prices.

Observe that an increase in the quantity of a good that

a person will buy at a certain price reflects an increase in the price that he will pay for a certain quantity of the good. Suppose at a specific time that a person would buy q_0 units of a good at the price p_0 and $q_0 + 1$ units of the good at a lower price p_1. Then at a later time he will buy $q_0 + 1$ units at p_0 if and only if he will now pay a price of p_0 for the additional unit. Thus the increase of one unit in his demand for the good on prices between p_1 and p_0 would reflect an increase of $p_0 - p_1$ units of money in the price at which he would buy that extra unit. Decreases in levels of demand similarly reflect decreases in the prices that people will pay for certain quantities of a good.

3.2   Direct Causes of Changes in the Supply of Goods

Levels of supply of a good change when the willingness and ability of people to sell units of it change. Like levels of demand, levels of supply need not rise or fall uniformly across all prices.

The willingness of a person to sell a unit of a good that he possesses or produces again reflects the value that he places on it relative to the values that he places on units of money in consideration of the ways in which he might dispense that money. When he places greater relative value on the unit, the supply of the good will fall on some prices; when he places less relative value on the unit, the supply of the good will rise on some prices. These values can change as his needs or wants change.

The ability of a person to sell a unit of a good reflects the quantity of the good that he possesses or produces because he can sell only materials that he owns or services that he provides. But once a person sells or consumes a unit of a good, he cannot sell it again; in order to sell another unit, he must first procure or produce another unit. Therefore, if a producer sells his good at a price where consumers will exhaust his stock within a certain period of time, then any difference between the numbers of units that he owns or provides in that period and in a subsequent one of the same length must result from a change in his rate of production of the good. When he produces the good at a higher rate, the supply of the good will rise from period to period; when he produces the good at a lower rate, the supply will fall.

3.3 Indirect Causes of Changes in the Demand for Goods

Changes in levels of demand, supply, or price can lead indirectly to changes in other levels of demand as they cause changes in the amounts of money that buyers possess. First, if the supply or demand for a good X falls at its current price and the seller of X fails to adjust that price in response, then normally some people will now purchase fewer units of X. The demand for other goods (especially those that serve the same purpose as X) that these people prefer should then rise on some prices because they will now have more money to spend on them (see section 3.1), though the demand for goods that they would use only in combination with X should fall on some prices. But these developments will not occur when the decrease in supply or demand eliminates a surplus or shortage. In this case, it should not induce any indirect changes in levels of demand.

Second, if the supply or demand for a good X rises at its current price and the seller of X fails to adjust that price in response, then normally no indirect changes in levels of demand will occur. But when the increase in supply or demand eliminates a shortage or surplus, some people will now purchase more units of X. The demand for other goods (especially those that serve the same purpose as X) that these people prefer should then fall on some prices because they will now have less money to spend on them, though the demand for goods that they would use only in combination with X should rise on some prices.

Third, if the seller of a good X lowers its price, then

some people will now purchase the same number of units of X that they would have purchased anyway but at less cost. The demand for other goods that these people prefer should then rise on some prices because they will now have more money to spend on them. But when the decrease in price eliminates or alleviates a surplus, other people will purchase more units of X than they would have purchased otherwise. The demand for other goods (especially those that serve the same purpose as X) that these people prefer should then fall on some prices because they will now have less money to spend on them, though the demand for goods they would use only in combination with X should rise on some prices.

Fourth, if the seller of a good X raises its price, then some people will purchase the same number of units of X that they would have purchased anyway but at a greater cost. The demand for other goods that these people prefer should then fall on some prices because they will have less money to spend on them. But when the increase in price causes or exacerbates a surplus, other people will purchase fewer units of X than they would have purchased otherwise. The demand for other goods (especially those that serve the same purpose as X) that these people prefer should then rise on some prices because they will now have more money to spend on them, though the demand for goods they would use only in combination with X should fall on some prices.

The earnings of the seller of a good will also change as the number of units that he sells and the price at which he sells them change. The demand for the goods that he himself prefers should then also rise or fall on some prices because he will now have more or less money to spend on them.

3.4 Indirect Causes of Changes in the Supply of Goods

Changes in levels of demand, supply, or price can also lead indirectly to changes in other levels of supply as they cause changes in revenues or expenses. First, if the demand for a good rises at its current price and the producer of the good raises that price to eliminate or alleviate the shortage that results, then he will earn greater revenue and profit on the sale of the same number of units of the good. If the demand for a good rises at its current price to eliminate or alleviate an existing surplus, then the producer will earn greater revenue and profit on the sale of a greater number of units of the good. Such increases in profit will tend to lead to higher rates of production and levels of supply of the good (see section 5.2).

Second, if the demand for a good falls at its current price and its producer lowers that price to eliminate or alleviate the surplus that results, then he will earn less revenue and profit on the sale of the same number of units of the good. If the demand for a good falls at its current price and its producer fails to lower that price to eliminate or alleviate a surplus that results, then he will earn less revenue and profit on the sale of a lesser number of units of the good. Such decreases in profit will tend to lead to lower rates of production and levels of supply of the good (see again section 5.2).

Third, if levels of demand or supply of the ingredients, labor, or plant required for the production of a good change at their current prices and the producers of the ingredients, labor, or plant adjust those prices to eliminate the shortages or surpluses that result, then the expenses of the producer of the good will also change. Lower expenses will then mean higher profits while higher expenses will mean lower profits. Such changes in profits will then induce the changes in rates of production and levels of supply of the good described above.

3.5 Effects of Changes in Population on Prices

Levels of supply of goods will rise or fall with rates of their production. Rates of production of goods will rise or fall with the number of producers in society, assuming rates of production per producer remain constant. And the number of producers in society will rise or fall with its population, assuming the number of producers per capita remain constant. Hence levels of supply of goods in a society will tend to rise when its population rises and fall when its population falls.

On the other hand, levels of demand for goods may or may not change as the population of society changes. If the quantity of money in a society remains constant, then each person will have less money to spend on average when the population rises and more money to spend when it falls. But if the proportions in which its members allocate money among specific goods remain constant as well, then more people will want to buy a particular good at a given fraction of the income per capita when the population rises and fewer people will want to do so when it falls. Together, these developments merely indicate that the demand for a good will be higher at a lower price or lower at a higher price after an increase or decrease in population; they do not lead to any conclusion on whether demand will rise or fall at a given price.

Nevertheless, if the proportions in which its members produce and consume units of specific goods also remain constant, then increases or decreases in levels of supply will ensure that buyers spend the same amounts of money in total for more units of goods after an increase in population and for fewer units of goods after a decrease in population. Therefore, prices of goods in a society will tend to fall when its population rises and rise when its population falls. More precisely, the reciprocal of any given price would change by the same percentage as the population if the proportions described remained constant so that an increase of $x\%$ in a population would cause a decrease of $100x/(100+x)\%$ in a price. While those assumptions of constancy indeed will never hold true, in the absence of additional information we must predicate any forecast of the impact of an increase or decrease in population on prices upon them.

3.6 Sequences of Changes in Demand, Supply, and Price

Changes in levels of demand, supply, and price will precipitate changes in other levels of demand, supply, and price, which will precipitate more changes, which will precipitate still more changes, and so forth. Thus a single change in a level of demand, supply, or price can initiate a lengthy sequence of changes in levels of demand, supply, and price, the scope and degree of which we cannot predict.

3.7 Measurability of Supply, Demand, and Price

While we cannot predict changes in levels of supply, demand, or price, a producer can normally measure levels of supply, levels of demand at prices of sale, and prices of sale themselves for his particular good over two periods of time in the past and calculate the differences between them; however, he cannot know the levels of demand for his good at prices other than that at which he sells it and will not be able to calculate the changes in such levels at those prices.

We also cannot measure degrees to which levels of supply, demand, and price have risen or fallen for all goods in general. A measurement of a general change in levels of supply or demand would require calculations of total numbers of units of all goods, but we cannot combine meaningfully quantities of disparate goods (see section 2.1). Similarly, a measurement of a general change in prices would require calculations of weighted averages of the prices of all goods, but no weighted average of prices can exist that will reflect the total cost of goods over a given period of time to more than one person because every person buys goods in a unique assortment and an increase or decrease in the price of a specific good will concern only those people who want to buy it. Hence we cannot calculate any single value that will summarize meaningfully for even two people (much less everyone) in society all changes in prices.

4

Investments

4.1 Savings

A person will accumulate *savings* when his earnings exceed his expenses and deplete savings when his expenses exceed his earnings. If he has no savings, then his expenses cannot exceed his earnings unless he receives charity or assumes debt. Though he must retain enough money at all times to pay for goods in quantities sufficient to meet his immediate needs and wants, the balance of his savings he can *invest*.

4.2 Investments

People invest money to accumulate more money. Kinds of investments include ownership of businesses, debt, and *commodities* (tangible goods that people buy and sell as investments). A person will gain money when his investment provides him with income but lose money when it encumbers him with expenses. An owner of a business gains income when he earns a profit on its operation. A lender gains income from the interest paid to him by a borrower. Holders of commodities earn no income from them, but do incur expenses to store and maintain them.

A person will also gain money when the price of his investment rises and lose money when it falls, though he will not realize the gain or loss until he sells the investment. Thus the total amount of money, realized or unrealized, that an investor will have gained from a unit of an investment over a period of time will equal the sum of the income (net of expenses) that he has derived from it and the appreciation in its price.

4.3   Prices of Investments

Levels of demand and supply determine values at which prices of investments reach equilibrium in the same way that they determine such values for goods. Levels of demand for an investment, like levels of demand for a good, reflect the willingness and ability of people to buy units of it (see section 3.1), which in turn depend upon the amounts of money that people possess, their needs and wants, their knowledge of other items (goods as well as other investments) available in the market, and the quality of the investment. Since people prefer to earn more money rather than less money, levels of demand for units of ownership of a business will tend to rise and fall with its profits.

Levels of supply of an investment, like levels of supply of a good, reflect the willingness and ability of people to sell units of it (see section 3.2). Units of ownership of businesses and units of debt of borrowers, unlike units of goods, neither vanish with consumption nor remain in perpetual production. Normally, the number of outstanding units of ownership in a particular company will increase only when its owners or directors issue and sell additional units (thereby diluting the equity in units) and decrease only when they buy and cancel existing units (thereby concentrating the equity in units). Similarly, the total number of outstanding units of debt of a particular producer or consumer will normally increase only when he assumes more debt and decrease only when he repays existing debt. Numbers of units of ownership of companies or debt of companies or individuals can also fall as a result of bankruptcy.

4.4   Yields and Returns on Investments

The annual *yield* on a unit of an investment is the quotient of the annual income paid to him who holds it and the current price at which he can sell it in the market. If the periodic income from an investment does not change, then its yield will fall when its price rises and rise when its price falls. The *nominal return* (or simply *return*) on a unit of an investment that its holder will have earned over a period of time will equal the quotient of his total gain (through both income and appreciation of price) from it over the period and its price at the beginning of the period, expressed as a percentage. Negative gains and returns reflect losses.

Since investors prefer investments that provide them with greater income over those that provide them with less income, prices of the former will tend to exceed prices of the latter (see section 4.3) and yields on all investments of comparable quality will tend to converge. If potential investors cannot find any investments on which they believe they can earn a positive return on their money, then they will spend it on goods or hold it in reserve instead. They will not deliberately exchange more money in the present for less money in the future.

4.5   Nominal Returns versus Real Returns

At any given time, an investor can sell a unit of an investment and buy goods with the proceeds. But the quantity of a particular good that he could have bought with the proceeds from its sale at the beginning of a period of time may differ from the quantity that he could have bought with the proceeds from its sale at the end of it. In terms of the good, his total gain over the period will equal the difference in these two quantities plus the quantities of the good that he could have bought periodically with his income (net of expenses) from the investment. His *real return* on the unit over the period with respect to the good will then equal the quotient of his total gain from the unit over the period in terms of the good and the quantity of the good that he could have bought with the proceeds from the sale of the unit at the beginning of the period, expressed as a percentage.

A nominal return measures the relative change in the monetary value of an investment, while a real return measures the relative change in the quantity of a good that the investment would afford its holder. On an investment with no yield, an investor will earn a positive nominal return but suffer a negative real return with respect to a good if the percentage by which the price of the investment has risen is less than the percentage by which the price of the good has risen. We can also apply the adjectives *nominal* and *real* to other monetary measures (such as wages, incomes, or profits) to differentiate between a relative change in the value of the measure and a relative change in the quantity of a good with monetary value equal to that of the measure.

5

Profits and Production

5.1 Causes of Changes in Profits

The profit of a producer will rise when his revenues rise or his expenses fall (see section 1.7). Assuming his rate of production remains constant, his revenues will rise when the demand for his good rises at its current price (see section 3.4). His expenses will fall when either the prices of the ingredients, labor, and plant that he uses fall (see again section 3.4) or he discovers a way to produce his good with a less costly combination of ingredients, labor, and plant. Conversely, the profit of a producer will fall when the demand for his good falls, the prices of the ingredients, labor, and plant that he uses rise, or his operation becomes less efficient.

A producer cannot assure himself of greater revenue and profit by simply raising the price of his good because the demand for the good at the higher price will be less than the demand for the good at the current price (see section 2.1). Hence the number of units of the good that he could sell would fall. If the decrease in sales were to outweigh the increase in price, then he would earn less revenue and profit, not more. For the same reason, a producer cannot maintain a certain level of profit in the face of rising expenses by simply "passing on" to consumers any increases in his costs of production.

5.2 Capitalizations and Tangible Assets of Businesses

The *capitalization* of a business is the product of the current price per share of ownership in the business and the total number of such shares outstanding. The *net value* of the tangible assets of a business is the sum of the current prices of those assets minus the liabilities of the business. The capitalization of a business will normally not deviate significantly from its net value. But if the profit of a business falls, then the price of its shares will fall with levels of demand for them (see section 4.3). Its capitalization may then fall below its net value. In such case the owners of the business will gain financially by terminating its operation, liquidating its assets, and placing the proceeds in investments that will provide them greater income. Hence businesses with capitalizations that lie below the net values of their tangible assets tend to disappear.

On the other hand, the price of the shares of a business will rise if its profit rises. Its capitalization may then rise above its net value. If its owners were then to replicate the business by investing and borrowing more funds in the same ratio of equity to debt and procuring, consuming, and engaging additional plant, ingredients, and labor in the same proportions, then not only would the cost of the expansion be less than the price at which the owners could sell it in the market, but also the quotient of the additional profit from the expansion and its cost would be greater than the quotient of the current profit of the business and its capitalization. Thus the owners would earn a relatively high return on investment in such expansion. While the return on the assets of the business would fall after the expansion of production (see section 5.4), the owners could continue to attract funds for even greater expansion as long as the yields that they could promise investors remained relatively high. Hence owners of businesses with capitalizations that lie above the net values of their tangible assets tend to expand their operations until the differences between those capitalizations and net values disappear.

5.3 Finance of Expansion of Production

To expand his operations, a producer may require more capital. He can finance the purchase of capital by tapping his own savings, assuming debt, or selling portions of ownership in his enterprise, but he cannot expand unless savings from some source avail for that purpose. In order to attract funds, he must offer to savers a yield on investment sufficiently high to outbid other producers who also seek those funds. A producer who foresees that he would earn relatively meagre profits on additional funds for capital will not even direct his own savings toward the expansion of his operations.

Rates of production that requires capital cannot increase in a society devoid of members willing to save money and defer consumption. Indeed, rates of such production will shrink in such a society because plant will deteriorate terminally without resources allocated for its repair. Nevertheless, greater savings do not always serve to expand or maintain the productive capacity of businesses. Purchases of outstanding shares of stock merely transfer ownership in a corporation, loans to consumers enable growth not in production but in consumption, and underground deposits of cash remain ineffectual until disinterred. Furthermore, any appropriation of money toward production of materials and services that do not satisfy the needs or wants of anyone will only serve to erode the wealth in society because such production will consume time and resources wastefully.

5.4 Effects of Expansion of Production

As a producer expands his operations and raises his rate of production, levels of supply of his good will rise (see section 3.2) as well as levels of demand for the ingredients, labor, and plant that he uses. The increases in supply will then cause the price of the good to fall, while the increases in demand will cause the prices of the ingredients, labor, and plant to rise. Consequently, his revenue per unit of the good will fall, his expenses per unit of the good will rise, and his profit per unit of the good will fall. As his profit per unit falls, the return on the assets of his business will also fall, assuming he has expanded his assets to the same extent that he has increased his production. Conversely, the profit per unit of a good and the return on the assets of the business of a producer will rise after he contracts his operations, assuming he has liquidated assets to the same extent that he has curtailed production.

The increases in levels of demand for ingredients, labor, and plant that accompany an increase in the rate of production of a good will also lead to increases in the profits of their producers, which will lead to increases in other levels of demand and profits, and so forth (see section 3.6). Since the producer that initially expanded production will normally have earned higher profits himself (see section 5.2) as a result of greater demand for his good or greater efficiency in production (see section 5.1), we may conclude that the profits on all materials and services that producers use either directly or indirectly in the manufacture of goods that come into greater favor with consumers or under more efficient production will tend to rise. Conversely, the profits on materials and services that producers use in the manufacture of goods that fall out of favor with consumers or under less efficient production will tend to fall, as well as the profits on those goods themselves.

A producer cannot always assure himself of a greater total profit by producing more units of a good because he would sell them at a lower profit per unit. He would also sell fewer units but at a higher profit per unit if he lowered his rate of production. In both cases his total profit could either be higher or lower than it was before, depending on whether or not the change in his profit per unit outweighed the change in the number of units he sold. Nevertheless, if the yield on the capitalization of a business is greater after expansion than before expansion, then the total profit of the business will also be greater after expansion than before expansion because the product of a higher yield and higher capitalization will be greater than the product of a lower yield and lower capitalization.

5.5   Effects of Changes in Ratios of Investment to Consumption

When people allocate greater portions of their incomes toward investment and lesser portions toward consumption, prices of investments will rise and prices of goods will fall with levels of demand for them. Hence prices of businesses (as investments) will rise and prices of the tangible assets (as goods) of businesses will fall. Thus capitalizations of businesses will rise above the net values of their tangible assets if they had been equal beforehand. Therefore, increases in funds for investment will not only enable (see section 5.3), but also encourage (see section 5.2) producers to expand their operations. Conversely, capitalizations of businesses will fall below the net values of their tangible assets and producers will terminate their operations when people save less and spend more money.

Changes in ratios of allocations toward investment to allocations toward consumption will affect not only prices of businesses, but also prices of debt; however, the latter will change more than the former. When these ratios rise, profits of businesses will fall as levels of demand for goods fall (see section 5.1), but payments of interest on debt will not change at all. Prices of debt will consequently rise more than prices of businesses because people prefer to earn more money rather than less money (see section 4.3) on their investments. When these ratios fall, profits of businesses will rise but payments of interest on debts will again remain unchanged; hence prices of debt will now fall more than prices of businesses.

OLSON

5.6   Effects of Changes in Population on Production

Prices of materials and services in a society will tend to fall
when its population rises and rise when its population falls
(see section 3.5). These changes will help people in some
ways, harm them in some ways, and affect them neutrally
in still other ways. With decreases in prices, people will
be able to buy goods in greater quantities with the cash
that they hold and in the same quantities with their wages,
but they will have greater difficulty discharging their debts
with their wages. With increases in prices, people must
buy goods in lower quantities with their savings in cash,
but they will be able buy goods in the same quantities and
discharge their debts more easily with their wages.

   While the effect on prices of a change in population will
thus prove neither wholly advantageous nor disadvanta-
geous, an increase in population will yield two unequiv-
ocally positive effects for all members of a society. First,
as people multiply they can divide the labor required for
production of goods more narrowly among themselves so
that each person can concentrate more of his own labor in
tasks at which he is most competent and leave more tasks at
which he is less competent to others to complete. As each
person produces a greater quantity of fewer goods (and
procures more goods through trade), rates of productivity
and quantities of intangible goods available in society for
consumption will rise. Moreover, these higher rates of productivity will allow producers of tangible goods to release
workers and spend more money on the same quantities of
ingredients and plant. The greater demand for ingredients
and plant will then lead sequentially to higher profits for
their producers, greater demand for raw materials, higher
profits for the producers of raw materials, greater production of raw materials, and greater production of tangible
goods (see sections 5.2 and 5.4).

   Second, as people fill the earth they will discover areas of the world in which they can extract minerals, grow

34

crops, or raise livestock of new kinds or in higher quantities.

Hence an increase in the population of a society will enable its members to produce goods in higher quantities per capita and in greater varieties and to meet thereby their needs and wants as consumers more adequately. Conversely, the members of society will meet their needs and wants less adequately as their number falls.

5.7 Production and Sacrifice

Rates of production of tangible goods per capita will rise only when people choose to invest more and consume less (see section 5.5), when the population rises (see section 5.6), when producers operate more efficiently (see sections 5.1 and 5.4), or when laborers work more hours. But each of these developments requires sacrifice and reduction of personal consumption. To invest more money, people must save greater portions of their incomes (see section 5.3). To expand a population, parents must spend greater portions of their incomes on children as they enlarge their families. To improve their efficiencies, producers must dedicate greater portions of their earnings toward newer plant, more advanced technologies, or the acquisition of higher skills. To work more hours, laborers must reduce their time of leisure.

Yet rates of consumption of tangible goods can rise only when rates of their production rise. Therefore, the members of society as a whole will enjoy greater material wealth in the future only when they forgo consumption in favor of greater investment in businesses or children in the present. Conversely, they will suffer greater deprivation of goods in the future when they eschew investment for greater personal consumption in the present.

6

Tendencies toward Prosperity

6.1 Motivation of Producers and Investors

To satisfy their physical needs and wants more adequately, people seek to consume goods of higher quality and in greater quantities. But in order to procure better goods or more goods, they must earn more money. Hence the desire for higher earnings prevails in all individuals who produce and the desire for higher returns prevails in all individuals who invest; workers seek jobs with high wages and leave jobs with low wages, entrepreneurs enter industries where businesses have high profits and owners contract businesses with low profits, and investors direct savings into investments with higher yields and out of investments with lower yields. Prospects of higher incomes will also induce people to work more hours and save more money.

6.2 Significance of Price, Profit, and Loss

Prices reach equilibrium at higher values when levels of demand rise or levels of supply fall and at lower values when levels of demand fall or levels of supply rise (see section 2.3). In other words, higher prices reflect greater demand relative to supply and lower prices reflect lesser demand relative to supply. Thus the price of a good at equilibrium measures the need of participants in the market for greater production of that good in comparison to other goods.

From this interpretation of price we can extract the significance of profit and loss to a society. The revenue that a producer earns from selling one unit of a good equals its price and the expense that he incurs in producing it equals the sum of the prices of the amounts of the ingredients, labor, and plant that he uses in its production. Therefore, a profit on operations indicates that a producer has transformed goods that the members of society need less into goods that they need more (assuming all prices have reached equilibrium). Likewise, a loss on operations indicates that a producer has destructively transformed goods that the members need more into goods that they need less.

As a comparison between sums of prices and a reflection of a change in profits, the difference between the capitalization of the business of a producer and the net value of its tangible assets also holds significance. When positive, the difference indicates that the members of society place higher values on his uses of the assets in collection than on other uses for them in separation and that further assembly of like resources for the same purpose will serve them well. When negative, the difference indicates that the producer underutilizes the assets under his control and that dissolution of his business (in part if not in whole) will beneficially liberate materials for other ends.

The degree of the need of the members of a society for greater production of a good may not reflect the degree of their need of the good for survival; while all people need clean water to survive, they may not need greater production of clean water if it already exists in plentiful supply. Yet in accordance with the right of each person in a free society to dispose of his property in the manner that he pleases, our measures of need for greater production of goods, namely prices at equilibrium, will reflect the preferences of consumers who can spend much money more than they reflect the preferences of consumers who can spend little money. Regardless of the fairness of this situation, no other means exist (or can exist) by which we can objectively appraise the need for production of a good.

6.3   The Invisible Hand

For the overall assortment of goods in existence to better satisfy the needs and wants of members of society, producers must direct more labor and ingredients into goods on which they earn higher wages and profits (see section 6.2), investors must direct more savings into capital for highly profitable producers (see section 5.3), and people generally must make the sacrifices required for greater production (see section 5.7).

But people naturally act in exactly this manner! High yields do induce investors to provide funds to producers for the right forms of plant, high profits and high wages do induce producers to deliver the right kinds of materials and labor to consumers, and prospects of higher incomes do induce people to work more hours and save more money because in every capacity people want more money with which to purchase goods that can satisfy their own needs and wants more adequately (see section 6.1). Thus individuals motivated by self-interest act to serve the other members of society without need for coercion or a central plan as prices and profits guide them to direct scarce resources into the production of goods that will satisfy their needs and wants optimally.

7

Money

7.1 Real and Substitutive Money

Two kinds of money exist: *real* and *substitutive*. Real money is a physical commodity. Substitutive money is a direct claim on real money that its issuer (normally a banker) promises to redeem upon the demand of its holder.

Substitutive money frees buyers and sellers from the carriage of unwieldy coins or packets of the monetary commodity. Hence greater amounts of real money will fall out of circulation and into storage as the use of substitutive money in a society grows. A banker may accept from his customers the substitutive money that another banker issues, but bankers will transfer real money between themselves periodically to reconcile net differences in the claims that they receive.

The prospect of greater wealth can tempt a banker to lend, invest, or spend real money on which he has issued substitutive money or issue substitutive money for which he holds no real money. By such artifice, bankers collectively can produce substitutive money in a quantity that far exceeds the quantity of the real money that undergirds it. But no banker can immediately redeem claims on real money that he does not hold. Hence substitutive money divides into two classes, *realizable* and *unrealizable*, that reflect whether its issuer can or cannot redeem it upon demand.

7.2 Inflation and Deflation

Monetary *inflation* is an increase and monetary *deflation* is a decrease in the total quantity of a money. An inflation must always precede a deflation. The quantity of a real money rises when its fabricator produces it and falls when people render it unusable for the purpose of exchange. The quantity of a substitutive money rises when a banker issues it and falls when he redeems it or annuls it in bankruptcy.

People can buy more goods with which to satisfy their needs and wants when they gain money but fewer goods when they lose it. Thus the real money in a society, if durable, will tend to accumulate over time. But substitutive money can disappear quickly when many depositors attempt simultaneously to withdraw funds from unsound banks. Once depositors withdraw all the real money from the coffers of a bank with inadequate reserves, the owner of the bank will not be able to satisfy outstanding claims on it. The unrealizable money that he has issued will then lose its value and disappear as the bank collapses.

7.3 Effects of an Inflation

7.3.1 Increases in Prices and Profits

When a person gains possession of more money, levels of demand for most goods and investments that he prefers will rise on some prices (see section 3.1). These increases in demand will then cause the prices of those goods and investments to reach equilibrium at higher values (see section 2.3). As the sellers of the goods and investments raise their prices accordingly, their revenues from sales will also rise. These increases in revenues in turn will cause levels of demand for most goods and investments that they prefer to rise, which will cause the prices of those goods and investments to rise, which will cause the revenues of the sellers of those goods and investments to rise, and so forth.

Thus greater production of a money, where not offset by destruction of or loss of access to the same amount of it, will cause prices of goods and investments to rise.

Some prices will rise earlier, and thus initially further, than others after an inflation. Prices of goods will tend to rise before the prices of the ingredients, labor, and plant used to produce them because levels of demand for the latter will rise only after the revenues of the sellers of the former rise. Prices of ingredients and labor will tend to rise before prices of plant because producers must buy new units of ingredients and labor continuously but need buy new units of plant only when old units of plant cease to function. And prices of ingredients will tend to rise before prices of labor because sellers of ingredients can recognize and respond to increases in levels of demand for their goods more quickly than sellers of labor; the seller of an ingredient can easily monitor the rate of sales of his good and raise his price if buyers exhaust his stock faster than he expects, but workers do not always actively market their services to potential buyers or gauge the demand for their labor, especially if they hold a salaried position in which they feel content. Therefore, prices of retail goods, ingredients, labor, delicate plant that needs frequent replacement, and durable plant that does not need frequent replacement will tend to rise in that order.

Prices of investments (especially those traded in heavy volume) will tend to rise even earlier than prices of goods after an inflation because astute speculators will anticipate its consequences, buy and sell investments quickly to gain from the developments they foresee, and force the prices of those investments to adjust to the new conditions in the market even before people alter their habits of spending; however, prices of investments, like prices of goods, will not all rise uniformly. The revenues of a producer will rise before his expenses because the price of his good will rise before the prices of the ingredients, labor, and plant that he needs. Thus his revenues will initially rise by a greater percentage than his expenses and his profits will rise by a greater percentage than his revenues. But since his revenues will rise by the same percentage as the price of his good, his profits then must rise by a greater percentage than the price of his good. Hence his profits will rise both in nominal terms and in real terms (relative to his own good). On the other hand, payments of interest on debt will remain constant. Therefore, in correspondence with levels of demand, prices of ownership of businesses will initially rise more than prices of both commodities (as goods) and debt because people prefer to earn more money rather than less money on their investments (see section 6.1).

Prices then will not vary directly with the quantity of money, but will react to an inflation in unpredictable ways and to different degrees. Nevertheless, the rate of inflation will serve both as a rough baseline about which rates of increase in prices will lie if the population of society remains constant and as our best forecast for the rate of increase in the price of any particular good if we cannot predict how other quantities that affect the price will change. Although the rate of increase in the price of a good may well deviate from this baseline for a short period of time, it cannot remain far above or below the rate of inflation in perpetuity because no price can exceed the total quantity of money and no producer can accept perennial losses on his production. Therefore, the rates of increase of all prices of goods will tend to approach the rate of inflation over a long period of time in a society with constant population and unimproved methods of production, provided those goods remain available.

7.3.2 Expansions of Businesses

An inflation will cause the capitalizations of businesses to rise before the net values of their tangible assets because it will cause the prices of investments to rise before the prices of plant (see subsection 7.3.1). But it will also cause the profits of businesses to rise in real terms (see again subsection 7.3.1). These increases in profits will motivate people to allocate greater portions of their incomes toward shares of ownership in businesses (and lesser portions toward goods or other investments) and will intensify the increases in levels of demand for such shares. Hence capitalizations of businesses will tend to rise substantially further than the net values of their tangible assets immediately after an inflation. Consequently, producers will seek to expand their businesses (see section 5.2).

As producers issue and sell shares of businesses or certificates of debt to secure funds for expansion, levels of supply of those investments will rise, levels of demand for other investments will fall (see section 3.3), and prices of investments in general will fall. As the producers then begin to spend those funds on new equipment and facilities, levels of demand and prices of plant will rise, as well as levels of demand for labor to construct and operate the facilities. Thus expansion will lead to decreases in capitalizations and increases in net values of tangible assets of businesses. Nevertheless, a producer will continue to expand until the capitalization and the net value of his own business reach equality.

7.3.3 Increases in Expenses

An inflation will cause the prices of goods to rise before the prices of the ingredients, labor, and plant used to produce them (see subsection 7.3.1). But as it stimulates people to allocate greater portions of their higher incomes toward investments in businesses and lesser portions toward goods for personal consumption, levels of demand for plant and labor will rise (see subsection 7.3.2) relative to levels of demand for goods of other kinds. Hence the prices of the plant and labor that producers need will eventually come to rise more than the prices of the goods that they sell, their expenses will come to rise more than their revenues, and their profits will come to fall in real terms below their levels at the time of the inflation.

These increases in expenses will affect adversely not only the profits of producers, but also the very projects of expansion that led to them. At the time that he decides to expand his operations, a producer will use current prices to estimate the cost of the project. He will then solicit funds in an amount sufficient to cover that cost. Although he may make some allowance for expenses that may exceed his estimates, he will not seek much more money than he believes he will need because he will want to minimize any debt, dilution of ownership, or depletion of personal savings that the acquisition of funds may require (see section 5.3). But simultaneous expansion by many producers can cause prices of plant and labor to rise significantly and unexpectedly in a short period of time. If they rise after the producer undertakes but before he completes his project, then he may discover that the funds he has secured cannot cover its cost. He will then need to raise more money, revise the project, or abandon it altogether. A producer who incurs debt to expand his facilities may have extreme difficulty even meeting his obligations to creditors because as long as the expansion remains incomplete, he will gain no additional revenues to offset his additional expenses for plant, labor, and interest.

7.3.4 Liquidations of Businesses

When the profits of businesses begin to fall (see subsection 7.3.3), people will begin to allocate smaller portions of their incomes toward ownership of businesses and larger portions toward goods, debt, and commodities. The prices of shares and capitalizations of businesses will then fall as levels of demand for the shares fall, but the prices of plant and the net values of the tangible assets of businesses will rise as levels of demand for materials rise. Since profits will eventually come to fall in real terms below their levels at the time of the inflation, the capitalizations of businesses will eventually fall below the net values of their tangible assets. The owners of some of the businesses will then choose to liquidate their assets and discontinue production (see section 5.2).

These liquidations will likely effectuate others. As an owner terminates the operation of his business, levels of demand for the ingredients and plant that he had required, the prices of those goods, and the revenues of their producers will fall in turn. The profits and capitalizations of the businesses of these producers will then fall further, leading some of them to discontinue production as well. Consequently, levels of demand for the ingredients and plant that they had required will fall, the profits and capitalizations of the businesses of their producers will fall further, some of them will discontinue production, and so forth. In such way chains of liquidations will radiate from one producer through many others.

Declines in the revenue and capitalization of a business cannot force its owner to liquidate it, but they will impair both his ability to pay the interest on his debt and the value of the collateral (namely the business itself) that supports the debt. If he defaults on his debt, then his creditors can force him to liquidate; indeed, they likely will do so quickly in order to minimize their own financial losses. Hence the percentage of businesses in society that fold after an inflation will correlate positively to the percentage of them with liabilities.

7.3.5 Losses to Investors

An inflation will induce producers to seek and investors to provide funds for the expansion of businesses when it causes the capitalizations of the businesses to rise to high levels (see subsection 7.3.2). But the prices of both shares in the ownership and certificates of the debt of a business will fall when its profit and the quality of its debt deteriorate (see subsection 7.3.4). Therefore, a person who enables an expansion shortly after an inflation by buying new shares or new debt of a business will likely see the price of his investment fall.

For similar reasons, a creditor who provides a loan to a consumer shortly after an inflation will likely see its price decline from its principal. As owners terminate the operations of their businesses or exhaust their funds for expansion, levels of demand for labor will fall. As the prices of labor (i.e., wages) fall in correspondence, workers will face greater difficulty in repaying their loans. Hence the quality of noncommercial loans will also deteriorate and their prices will follow suit.

Losses on depreciated investments can often remain unrealized until their holders choose to sell them (see section 4.2); however, creditors can force a producer or consumer to liquidate his business or his assets if he defaults on a loan (see subsection 7.3.4). Greater liquidation of businesses will then lead to greater decreases in profits and wages, greater losses on investments, and greater insolvency among other producers and consumers. Investors in the financial instruments of an insolvent entity who do not have a preferential claim on the proceeds from its liquidation can suffer severe losses on their investments.

7.3.6 Destruction of Unrealizable Money

Creditors who lend their own money to debtors will bear alone any costs of their errors in judgment, but those who lend and lose money that they themselves had borrowed will pass the losses onto their own creditors. In particular, a default on debt may leave the owner of a bank unable to discharge his own liabilities to depositors or other holders of his substitutive money. But once a banker refuses to honor a demand to redeem units of substitutive money that he has issued, he will trigger an avalanche of similar demands for redemptions as the fear of losing their money spreads first to his other creditors and then to the creditors of other local bankers. Upon exposure of their insolvency, the least sound of the banks will collapse and the quantity of substitutive money in society will fall as realizable money meets redemption and unrealizable money disappears. As the total quantity of money in the society falls, its members will suffer the effects of a deflation. The prices of assets and the wages of debtors will fall (see section 7.4), the quality of the balance sheets of other banks will deteriorate, more banks will collapse, the quantity of substitutive money will fall further, and so forth. The process will end with the total destruction of the unrealizable money in society.

7.4 Effects of a Deflation

A deflation will generally affect prices, profits, and production in ways opposite those in which an inflation affects them (see section 7.3). As the quantity of money in existence falls, prices of retail goods, ingredients, labor, delicate plant that needs frequent replacement, and durable plant that does not need frequent replacement will fall in that order, though prices of labor should change more quickly after a deflation than after an inflation because businessmen will recognize immediately their need to reduce the wages that they offer workers when their revenues shrink. As prices of goods fall, profits of businesses will fall by an even greater percentage, prices of ownership of businesses will fall more than prices of commodities and debt, and capitalizations of businesses will fall before the net values of their tangible assets. The owners of some businesses will then choose to liquidate them (see section 5.2), liquidations will lead to more liquidations (see subsection 7.3.4), and rates of production of goods will fall further.

7.5 Recovery of Profits and Rates of Production

Though the profits of businesses will rise immediately after an inflation (see subsection 7.3.1), both profits and rates of production of goods will eventually begin to fall (see subsection 7.3.4). If unrealizable money exists in the society, those profits and rates will continue to fall during the consequent deflation (see section 7.4). But as the quantity of money in the society stabilizes, the rate of liquidations of businesses will subside to a normal level and rates of production will reach their nadirs.

At this point in time, only businesses in strong financial condition will remain in operation. In fact, the condition of a producer who avoids liquidation may improve through a deflation because failures of his competitors will lead not only to decreases in levels of demand for the ingredients, labor, and plant that he requires (see subsections 7.3.4 and 7.3.5), but also to increases in levels of demand for the good that he himself produces (see section 3.3). As prices of the former fall and the price of the latter rises consequently, his expenses will fall, his revenues will rise, and his profit will rise. Once profits rise sufficiently far, opportunities for high returns will again induce investors to furnish funds to businessmen for expansion and rates of production will rebound higher.

8

The Economic Cycle

8.1 Cycle of Economic Activity

We may summarize the effects of an inflation as a cycle of expansion, contraction, and recovery. In the stage of expansion, profits of businesses and prices of labor will rise (see subsections 7.3.1 to 7.3.2) and the members of society will feel wealthier. In the stage of contraction, profits, wages, and production will fall (see subsections 7.3.3 to 7.3.5) and the members of society will be poorer. If delinquencies on debt induce a deflation (see subsection 7.3.6), then profits and wages will fall even further (see section 7.4), where the severity of the depression will depend upon the amount of money that disappears. In the stage of recovery, rates of production of goods will rise (see section 7.5), though not necessarily beyond the rates that producers maintained before the expansion. At the conclusion of the stage of recovery, the economic cycle will terminate absent additional production of money.

Pressure from creditors and insolvencies of banks will ensure that a deflation expunges unrealizable money both quickly (see subsection 7.3.4) and thoroughly (see subsection 7.3.6). Thus an inflation of unrealizable money, which must eventually disappear, will lead to a sharper, shorter, and fuller economic contraction than will an inflation of an equivalent amount of real money, which may never disappear. Yet liquidations of assets of unprofitable businesses, purgation of debt, and eradication of excessive new units of money cleanse the market of unjustifiable production and allow worthwhile production to return to levels at which the assortment of goods available in society optimally satisfy the needs and wants of consumers. Hence a shorter but deeper contraction after an inflation, though more painful in the near term, will affect the wealth of the members of society more positively in the long run than one less so.

8.2   Inflation to Prolong Expansion and Avert Contraction

When the real money of a society consists of a material that allows its fabricator to produce it in arbitrarily high quantities at no extra cost, he can attempt to prolong a stage of expansion and circumvent a stage of contraction within an economic cycle by inflating the stock of money further. But though a finite number of additional acts of inflation can indeed magnify in size, scope, or duration the temporary increases in real profits of businesses that a first act causes, they will also lead to greater expansion of facilities for production and greater increases in the expenses of producers relative to their revenues (see subsection 7.3.3). Hence such additional inflation would ultimately cause profits, capitalizations, wages, and production to fall even further in the latter stages of the cycle.

Perpetual inflation likewise will not circumvent an economic contraction. Chronic increases in the quantity of money will lead to chronic increases in the prices of goods, which will require investors to earn higher nominal yields on their investments in order to earn the same real returns. Thus prices of investments will fall (see section 4.4) relative to incomes from investments and prices of goods. Consequently the capitalizations of businesses will fall below the net values of their tangible assets if they had been equal beforehand, their owners will terminate their operations (see section 5.2), and production will again contract.

8.3 Extension and Repetition of the Economic Cycle

Additional inflation cannot prevent the economic contraction to which an initial inflation must lead (see section 8.2), but it can mitigate the effects of a deflation; if the quantity of real money in a society rises while the quantity of unrealizable money falls, then the effects of the increase will counteract the effects of the decrease to some extent. Yet such counteractive measures will merely slow the rates of liquidations of assets, purgation of debt, and eradication of excessive new money (see section 8.1). In other words, such inflation will delay the correction of imbalances in allocations of scarce resources between plant for production and goods for consumption, inhibit the recovery of rates of production to levels that correspond more closely to the needs and wants of consumers, and extend the period of greater material deprivation of the members of the society.

In fact, production of real money that counteracts destruction of unrealizable substitutive money will not only extend the length of an economic cycle, but will ensure a retracement through its phases. A deflation will cause borrowers and bankers to suffer losses of collateral and reputation and will cause depositors to suffer losses of savings as it leads to delinquencies on debt and failures of banks (see subsection 7.3.6). These losses will then discourage people from borrowing and lending money through banks and encourage bankers to scrutinize applications for loans more carefully in the future. By forestalling such losses, an arrest of a deflation will leave borrowers more willing to assume debt, savers more willing to deposit their money in banks, and bankers less motivated to tighten the standards against which they underwrite loans. Thus counteraction of destruction of unrealizable money will facilitate further production of it.

But further production of unrealizable money will initiate another sequence of expansion and contraction. The producer of real money could then counteract the eventual deflation again, but in doing so he would simultaneously enable and encourage bankers to produce more unrealizable money again. As long as bankers continue to produce more unrealizable money and the producer of real money continues to counteract its destruction, the total quantity of money and the prices of goods in society will ratchet ever higher, economic activity will alternately intensify and slacken, and profits and wages will alternately rise and fall in real terms.

8.4 Destruction of Real Money

A persistently high or ever rising rate of increase in the quantity of a money will lead to high rates of increase in prices and will induce people to dishoard it in favor of tangible goods or another money. As long as the rate of inflation in a society remains high, the average length of time for which its members hold the depreciating currency will continue to shorten. Eventually they will abandon it altogether and all savings in the money will become worthless. Until a new money can gain acceptance in the society, all trade will take the form of barter, all specialization of labor will disappear, and its members will live more primitively.

8.5 Beneficiaries of Inflation and Deflation

An inflation or deflation will help a person to the extent that it causes the wages from his labor, the balances on his savings, the prices of his assets, and the earnings from his investments to rise more or fall less than the payments on his liabilities and the prices of the goods he wants to buy, but will harm him to the extent that it causes the former to rise less or fall more than the latter. Hence an inflation will tend to strengthen the financial conditions of people who have assumed debt while a deflation will tend to weaken them. Indeed, a deflation can cause wages and prices to fall to levels so low that debtors will never be able to repay their creditors and will effectively become permanent slaves to them.

Since people spread their money across multiple sellers as they buy various items, an inflation will cause the wealth of the producer of the money (its primary recipient) to rise more than that of the sellers of the goods and investments that he prefers (the secondary recipients), their wealth to rise more than that of the sellers of the goods and investments that they prefer (the tertiary recipients), and so forth. Thus the production of money will have the greatest positive impact on the person who produces it. For similar reasons, the destruction of money will have the greatest negative impact on the person who loses it. In general, an inflation will tend to affect most negatively people who maintain fixed incomes and hold their savings in cash, but a deflation will affect the same people most positively.

8.6   Effects of Inflation and Deflation on Overall Production

While an inflation of real money will bestow permanent financial gains and losses on some people because it seldom disappears (see section 7.2), a corrective deflation can negate some of the effects of an inflation of substitutive money. Yet no combination of doses of inflation and deflation will affect any member of society in a perfectly neutral way. In fact, an inflation must affect the members of society negatively on average because the quantities of goods available for them to consume will fall throughout most of the economic cycle that it triggers; producers will divert labor and materials out of goods for consumption and into plant (see subsection 7.3.2) in the stage of expansion and will shutter their operations (see subsection 7.3.4) in the stage of contraction. While quantities of goods for consumption will rise in the stage of recovery (see section 7.5), we cannot expect them to rise beyond their levels before the inflation to compensate for the losses within the cycle.

Furthermore, the efforts that producers make toward

expansion in the early stages of the economic cycle will never actually lead to greater material wealth. Those who can complete their construction of new facilities will raise their rates of production only at unexpectedly high costs and for unexpectedly low yields, and those who begin but fail to complete such construction or who liquidate their facilities shortly after they construct them will only squander the labor and materials they used in the endeavors. In both cases the size of the financial losses that investors in the expansions suffer will reflect the degree of waste of resources that they have enabled through their misdirection of funds, and the negativity of the losses will indicate that such attempts at expansion will not have served the members of society beneficially (see section 6.2). Not only investors, but all members of society will suffer the costs of reductions in consumable goods that such waste will necessitate.

An inflation can never actuate greater overall production of tangible goods because it will not stimulate the members of society to save more and spend less of their money. Indeed, depreciation of the money of society will only encourage its members to deplete and expend their savings. If savers perceive that the quantities of goods that they can buy with a unit of the money will fall and that investments in businesses will generate negative real returns, then they will liquidate such investments, minimize the amounts of cash they hold, and exchange any money that they acquire in excess of these minimums for goods or harder monies. But lesser savings and investment not only will fail to lead to higher rates of production and consumption, they also must lead to lower rates of production and consumption (see section 5.7). Thus an inflation that causes prices to rise must lead to material deprivation, a greater inflation to greater material deprivation (see section 8.3), and an extreme inflation to widespread material devastation (see section 8.4).

9

Avoidance of Crisis

9.1 Constraints on Inflation of Real Money

As a producer of real money inflates its supply, the prices of the ingredients, labor, and plant that he requires for its production will rise (see subsection 7.3.1). Consequently his expenses will rise and his profit will fall. His profit will approach zero units of money as his cost to produce one unit of money approaches one unit of money, but he will terminate production before his profit turns negative. Hence prices themselves will naturally constrain the inflation of real money. While prices would fail to constrain the inflation if the real money cost nothing to produce because the profit to its producer then would need never decline, the members of a society will not normally accept a costless real money as payment for goods because they know that its producer will eventually depreciate it unto oblivion.

9.2 Constraints on Inflation of Substitutive Money

People normally will accept costless claims on real money as payment for goods. Yet they will do so only as long as the rate of production of those claims does not exceed the constrained rate of production of the real money that undergirds them (see section 9.1). They will reject a substitutive money if they discover that its producer has issued it in excess and cannot fulfill his obligation to redeem it (see subsection 7.3.6).

Indeed, the risk of losing money in the collapse of a bank will provide incentive for individuals (especially rival bankers) who hold claims on real money issued through it to monitor its financial condition closely. They will rush to redeem those claims at the first sign of its insolvency and will compel its liquidation to recover the funds due them if its reserves prove insufficient to meet its obligations. The celerity with which the members of society would expose and expurgate fraudulent practices will in fact force bankers to match the terms of the loans they make to the terms of the nondemandable deposits they take and to keep the ratios of the amounts of real money they hold in reserve to the amounts of substitutive money they issue above one. In order to maintain a level of reserves sufficient to cover all their immediate obligations, they will need to transfer real money from circulation to storage in the amounts of the claims they issue and from storage to circulation in the amounts of the claims they redeem.

Therefore, in a free society the total quantity of unrealizable substitutive money in existence will be negligible and the total quantity of realizable substitutive money in existence will rise and fall only as the quantity of real money in circulation changes by the same magnitude in the opposite direction. The rate of change of the total quantity of money (real and substitutive) in circulation will thus equal the rate of change of the quantity of real money in existence.

9.3 Intermittent Production of Money

Although prices will continue to fluctuate during a suspension of production of real money, they will fall universally only if the population of society rises (see section 3.5). The projected expenses of the producer of the money under a resumption of his operations would then also fall and his projected profit would rise. If the prices of the ingredients, labor, and plant that he would use were to fall and his projected profit were to rise sufficiently far, then he will resume his operations. Prices will then reverse course and begin to rise, but he will continue production until they rose to the point at which his profit had again drawn sufficiently close to zero (see section 9.1).

9.4 Expected Rate of Inflation

The profit that a producer earns on the production of one unit of real money will depend entirely on the expense of its production because his revenue from its production will always equal one unit of money. So if a producer of real money suspends his operations, then resumes them, and then suspends them again when his profit per unit has fallen to the same level at which he had suspended them previously (see section 9.3), then at the time of the second suspension his expense per unit will also have returned to the level it assumed at the time of the first suspension. If he has made no improvements in his methods of production in the interim, then the prices of the ingredients, labor, and plant that he uses will have returned to their former levels as well. But an increase of $x\%$ in the population will cause prices in general to fall by $100x/(100 + x)\%$ (see section 3.5), only an increase of $x\%$ in a price will counter a earlier decrease of $100x/(100 + x)\%$ in that price, and only an increase of $x\%$ in the quantity of real money will allow us to forecast an increase of $x\%$ in prices (see subsection 7.3.1). Therefore, we should expect a producer of real money to continue operations after a suspension until the quantity of money has risen by the same percentage that the population has risen from the time of the suspension, and then suspend them again. In other words, we may expect an increase of $x\%$ in the population between points of suspension of the production of real money to lead to an increase of $x\%$ in the quantity of the money.

Yet producers may well improve their operations. The discovery of a more efficient method of production will allow a producer of real money to mint more units than a reduction in prices alone would allow because his expenses will then fall further than they would have fallen without the discovery (see section 5.1). Hence we should expect the quantity of money in a society to ultimately rise by a slightly greater percentage than its population. A decrease in a population, absent any improvements in efficiencies, will lead to a permanent termination of the production of money.

9.5 Continuous Production of Money

While an increase slightly greater than $x\%$ in the quantity of a real money will follow an increase of $x\%$ in a population between points of suspension of intermittent production of the money (see section 9.4), it will also follow an increase of $x\%$ in the population between any two points in time under continuous production of the money because increases or decreases in population will still leave prices lower or higher than they would have been otherwise. Indeed, the production of real money normally will not cease; if multiple people produce the real money of a society, then the termination of the operations of one of them will still leave others in business, and if only one person produces it, then he will prefer to avoid disruption in his operations and will regulate his rate of production accordingly. Thus we should expect the periodic rate of inflation in a society to slightly exceed the periodic rate of growth of its population, with fluctuations in the former trailing fluctuations in the latter.

9.6 Stability of Prices

A producer of real money will inflate its supply at a rate sufficient to counter the decreases in his expenses (see section 9.4). But we should not expect increases in population or discoveries of more economical processes of production to lower the expenses of certain producers (such as the producer of real money) any more or less than they lower those of other producers. In general then, the inflation will tend to keep the expenses of all producers stable.

On the other hand, the inflation will tend to raise prices and the revenues of producers because it will counter not only the decreases in prices that result from an increase in population, but also the effects of greater economy in production. By raising revenues and keeping expenses constant, the production of money will thus preserve any increases in the profits of producers that improvements in their efficiencies may have rendered. These increases in profits will then induce them to expand their operations, causing the prices of their goods and the revenues and profits on their production to fall, until the returns on the tangible assets of their businesses return to the levels they assumed before expansion (see sections 5.2 and 5.4).

But we should expect the return on the assets of a producer to reach the level it had assumed earlier (that is, before the inflation and operational improvements) when the price of his good reaches the level it had assumed then. If the prices of all goods ultimately rise by inflation of money and fall by expansion of production by the same percentage (see subsection 7.3.1), producers maintain the same ratios of equity to debt, and the quantities of assets of producers grow proportionally to their rates of production (see section 5.2), then the revenue per unit and the net value of the assets per unit of production of a producer, which will then merely reflect the price of his good and the prices of his assets, respectively, will also ultimately change by the same percentage. Yet if these quantities change by the same percentage while the expense per unit of the producer remains constant, then the return on the tangible assets of the producer (that is, the quotient of the difference of his revenue per unit and expense per unit and the net value of his tangible assets per unit) will fall to its former level only when his revenue per unit and the net value of his assets per unit also fall to their former levels. Since the revenue per unit of a producer is equivalent to the price of his good, the price of his good will then also have fallen back to its former level at this point in time. Thus we should expect quantities of goods and the quantity of real money in a free society to grow at rates that keep prices stable.

9.7   The Optimum Quantity of Money

Without money, people cannot easily improve their conditions through exchange and must live primitively (see section 1.4). But once the members of society adopt a money of sufficient quantity, a decrease or increase of that money will normally lead to greater material deprivation for some or all of them (see section 8.5). A deflation will lead to liquidations of businesses (see section 7.4), an insignificant inflation that permits wages to fall will allow the financial condition of debtors to weaken, and a significant inflation that causes prices to rise will induce wasteful diversion of resources into expansion of businesses (see section 8.6).

On the other hand, changes in profits will reflect genuine changes in the preferences of consumers, allow producers and investors to accurately forecast financial returns on current businesses and potential projects, induce appropriate expansion or liquidation, and facilitate the accumulation of wealth when prices remain stable. Furthermore, constancy in prices will deny the unexpected disadvantage to debtors or creditors that a decrease or increase in wages and prices would bring. Therefore, only at a rate that stabilizes prices will the production of money benignly enable the members of society to maximize their material wealth overall.

But the quantity of real money in existence, as well as the total quantity of money in circulation (see section 9.2), in a free society will indeed rise at exactly this optimal rate (see section 9.6)! While no person can contrive effectively to keep prices stable because no person can measure meaningfully the general extent by which they have changed (see section 3.7), producers of money will naturally regulate their rates of production to a degree that secures this outcome. Thus we find again that prices and profits will guide the members of society to produce a good (namely money) in an optimal quantity without the need for coercion (see section 6.3).

PART II

Coercion

10

Kinds of Coercion

10.1 Controllers

Heretofore we have developed economic theory under an assumption that individuals retain inviolate rights on their selves and property. We will now examine the economic effects of coercion. We will define the term *controller* to mean anyone who uses force, whether directly or through subordinates, to take full or partial control of the person or property of someone else. A controller may operate in service to an organization (especially a government) or on his own behalf.

Violent action divides the members of society into two classes: those who benefit from the action and those who do not. Different acts of violence committed by the same controller can benefit different sets of people; the only person necessarily common to all sets is the controller himself, who will derive usually a material benefit and always a psychic benefit from his exercise of control. While violent action can sometimes help a majority of the members of society at the expense of a minority, it can never help all at the expense of none because every act of violence harms someone.

10.2 Destruction

A controller can injure people or their property by assault, murder, vandalism, arson, or other means. He may gain a psychic benefit from such action, but his victim will suffer some loss of health, property, or peace of mind. A third party (such as an insurer) may also bear a cost for any reparation that damage may warrant.

In most societies, multiple controllers exert power over the people. Often controllers will cooperate and share command peaceably in such situations, but sometimes they will disagree and engage in battle to maintain or enlarge their jurisdictions. As they inflict violence upon each other, they may destroy the lives and property of innocent people as well.

Controllers of large territories can also feign disagreement with each other and use war to reduce or purge their populations, though they can act unilaterally toward these ends as well by developing and spreading fatal diseases (while concealing their cures), terminating (or promoting the termination of) pregnancies, or sterilizing prospective mothers. Nevertheless, a controller cannot eliminate everyone under his control because he needs some people to serve him.

10.3 Seizure

A controller can seize, kidnap, and imprison people. Both captor and captive will usually suffer loss on an imprisonment; the former must spend money to meet the needs of the latter and the latter will lose his freedom. Nevertheless, the controller will gain a psychic benefit from incarcerating another human being and may eventually gain a material benefit if he can collect a ransom in return for the prisoner. In exceptional circumstances, the prisoner himself may gain by his detention if he prefers conditions inside his cage to conditions outside it.

A controller can also steal property from people. Controllers not in government tend to steal irregularly, while controllers in government steal regularly and systematically in the name of taxation. Forms of theft include:

- irregular seizure of property (e.g., illegal theft or confiscation through *eminent domain*)
- taxes on revenues from sales (e.g., taxes on *sales, personal incomes, financial transactions, imports,* or *exports*)
- taxes on profits from sales (e.g., taxes on *gains on investments, corporate incomes,* or *values added*)
- taxes on quantities of goods sold (e.g., *excises*)
- taxes on appraised values of property (e.g., taxes on *property, wealth, inheritances,* or *expatriation*)
- taxes of fixed amounts of money per *head*

A controller harms people from whom he takes property, though he can often persuade his victims to surrender their money without complaint by subtly perverting the language they use. By constantly asserting that his victims "owe" him all that he demands and labeling as "cheats" those who fail to pay him that tribute, he can cause some of them to feel guilty about retaining their own money.

In some cases of seizure, we can easily misidentify the victim. A tax on the sale of a good presents us with two parties who can plausibly claim our sympathies. Yet the tax directly harms the seller, not the buyer, of the good. The implementation of the tax will not alter the schedule of demand for the good or the value at which its price reaches equilibrium, so if the seller wishes to avoid a surplus, he must reduce the listed price of his good to the point at which the sum of that price and the tax (i.e., the total cost to buyers) equals the value of the price at equilibrium. Since the seller must pay the tax out of his receipts, it will reduce his profit directly. This principle applies to labor as much as any good (see section 2.2); hence employees (as sellers of labor), not employers (as buyers of labor), bear the cost of all taxes on wages.

We can also underestimate the degree of victimization in a seizure. When a controller establishes periodic taxes on a piece of property, not only does he extract wealth from its holder, but also he effectively assumes its ownership. Such taxes relegate the nominal owner of the property to the position of renter and elevate the controller to the position of landlord because the former must now remit periodic payment to the latter in order to retain control of it.

In fact, degrees of victimization can subtlely change without alteration of a schedule of seizure. If a controller assesses taxes on incomes, revenues, or profits at graduated rates that rise with the monetary values of such gains, then an inflation of money will also inflate the proportion of wealth that he seizes. An inflation may even allow a controller to collect money in taxes on nominal gains from investments that disguise real losses.

10.4 Controls on Prices

A controller can establish upper or lower limits on prices of goods or rates of interest.

10.4.1 Ceilings on Prices

A *ceiling* is an arbitrary upper limit on the price at which a controller allows a person to sell units of a good. A ceiling may not be effective; if it lies above the value at which the price of the good reaches equilibrium, then it will impose no burden on buyers or sellers. But a shortage of a good will exist at the maximum price established by an effective ceiling because the demand for the good will exceed the supply there. The severity of the shortage will depend upon the size of the discrepancy between the ceiling and the value at which the price of the good would have reached equilibrium.

Shortages require that someone decide who may buy and who may not buy units of goods. A controller may allow the seller of a good in shortage to make these decisions or he may arrogate the task to himself. Conventionally, sellers grant rights of purchase on a "first-come, first-served" basis or by lot, whereas controllers grant them to the politically connected elite of society. Regardless of the basis for such a decision and in contrast to a freely fluctuating price that will automatically guide units of a good into the hands of those who need them most urgently, neither a seller nor a controller can allocate with proper priority the units of a good in shortage because none can measure and compare rationally the degrees to which buyers need it.

An effective ceiling may help some potential buyers of the good affected but it must harm others. The ceiling will keep the price of units of the good artificially low and may allow some people to buy them for less money; however, the shortage that results will prevent other people who would have bought them at their price at equilibrium from buying them at any price. A potential buyer who cannot procure a unit of the good will suffer the most harm when he needs it for survival and no close substitutes for it exist. By imposing low ceilings on the prices of food, a controller can cause extreme shortages that result in mass starvation.

An effective ceiling will also harm the seller of the good affected because lower prices will bring him lower revenues and profits. If he curtails his operations because he can no longer earn a sufficiently high profit, then he will exacerbate the existing shortage further. A low ceiling that causes him to terminate his operations completely will harm not only the seller, but also all potential buyers of that good.

10.4.2 Floors on Prices

A *floor* is an arbitrary lower limit on the price at which a controller allows a producer to sell units of a good. A floor will not be effective if it lies below the value at which the price of the good reaches equilibrium. But a surplus of a good will exist at the minimum price established by an effective floor because the supply of the good will exceed the demand there. The severity of the surplus will depend upon the size of the discrepancy between the floor and the value at which the price of the good would have reached equilibrium; however, any surplus will prove temporary because people will not continue to produce excess units that they cannot sell.

An effective floor will harm all potential buyers of the good affected. It will keep the price of units of the good artificially high and force those who would have bought them at their price at equilibrium to either spend more money or forgo some satisfaction of their consumptive needs.

An effective floor can either help or harm the seller of the good affected. He will sell fewer units with the floor, but at a higher price per unit. If the increase in price were to outweigh the decrease in quantity sold, then his total profit will rise; if the decrease in quantity sold were to outweigh the increase in price, then his total profit will fall. Nevertheless, we can expect a floor to harm a seller in most cases because he would have reduced his level of production and raised the price of his good voluntarily otherwise. A high floor at which the demand for the good is zero will certainly harm him.

A *minimum wage* is a floor on the price of labor. An effective minimum wage will idle workers and reduce the quantities of goods that members of the society produce in total. As it forces people to produce less, it will simultaneously force them to consume less and prevent them from satisfying as many of their needs and wants as they could have otherwise; however, it will also ensure that juveniles have more time to snort drugs, deface buildings with graffiti, and plan violent attacks on others.

10.4.3 Controls on Rates of Interest

A ceiling or a floor on a rate of interest is equivalent to a floor or a ceiling, respectively, on the price of a certificate of debt. Therefore, an effective ceiling on a rate of interest will lead to a surplus of the certificates affected and will harm their potential buyers, but it can either help or harm their sellers. On the other hand, an effective floor on a rate of interest will lead to a shortage of the certificates affected and will harm their sellers, but it can either help or harm a potential buyer.

10.5   Controls on Exchanges

10.5.1   Depression and Elevation of Supply

A controller can prohibit a producer from selling a good in quantities above some upper limit (often zero units). Such a limit will cause levels of supply of the good to fall and its price to reach equilibrium at a higher value. The limit will harm all potential buyers of the good by forcing them to spend more money on it or forgo some satisfaction of their needs. It will also harm the potential seller of the good by preventing him from engaging in activity that will maximize his profit.

Conversely, a controller can compel a person to expend labor and resources to produce a good in greater quantities. An act of such compulsion will cause levels of supply of the good to rise and its price to reach equilibrium at a lower value. The act will help buyers of the good by allowing them to spend less money on it, but it will harm the slave by preventing him from deploying his labor and resources in ways more profitable to him.

10.5.2   Depression and Elevation of Demand

A controller can also prohibit consumers from purchasing a good in quantities above some upper limit (often zero units). Such a restriction will cause levels of demand for the good to fall and its price to reach equilibrium at a lower value. The restriction will harm the seller of the good by reducing his sales, revenues, and profits, and it will harm those who cannot now buy the good in the quantities they desire by preventing them from making exchanges that would improve their conditions. While the restriction may help those who would buy the good in quantities below the limit by causing its price to fall, this advantage will prove temporary if the seller eventually curtails his production in response to the drop in his profits and the price of the good subsequently rises.

Conversely, a controller can compel people to buy a good. An act of such compulsion will cause levels of demand for the good to rise and its price to reach equilibrium at a higher value. The act will help the seller of the good by raising his revenues and profits, but it will harm buyers of the good by forcing them to spend (more) money on the good that they could otherwise have spent on goods that would better satisfy their needs.

10.5.3 Regulations on Production

A controller can force producers to follow certain rules (beyond those that proscribe violations of rights on property) in order to sell their goods. A *regulation* will usually harm producers whose practices do not already conform to it if compliance requires them to expend time or money. It will also harm consumers if it denies them the opportunity to buy products that would meet their own standards and help to fulfill their needs. On the other hand, a regulation can help a producer, even when it costs him money in the short term, if it places a relatively greater burden on his competitors and eventually forces them out of business. A regulation that costs all producers the same amount of money will usually harm those who earn higher revenues less acutely than those who earn lower revenues.

Standards of quality on goods do not fail to exist in the absence of an idealistic controller, but they develop in accordance with the needs and wants of the populace. Consumers effectively impose conditions on producers when they select or avoid goods to buy because levels of demand for the goods of producers who voluntarily meet the conditions of consumers most satisfactorily tend to rise while levels of demand for the goods of producers who do not meet those conditions tend to fall. Over time, goods become more durable, more reliable, and less hazardous. Ironically, goods can become less durable, less reliable, or more hazardous after controllers enact standards for these qualities if consumers then assume that all products meet those standards and inspect them less diligently or if burdensome costs of proving adherence to those standards drive producers of goods of high quality out of business.

10.6 Claims to Land

A controller can claim ownership of all unused land within his territory. He can then sell portions of the land to individuals who will put them to productive use, allocate portions to allies who will rent them to tenants, or set portions aside permanently as refuges for wildlife or parks for temporary public visitation. Controllers often establish large parks or refuges next to their own homes to prevent ignoble elements of the population from erecting their own domiciles near them.

Appropriation of unused land will harm people who would extract minerals, grow crops, raise livestock, or build homes there by forcing them to pay the controller for the right to do so or by preventing its occupancy altogether. Such usurpation will help a controller by enabling him to gain money from its sale, favor from his allies, or distance from the rabble.

10.7 Monopoly

A controller may apply some of the money he seizes toward capital for his own commercial enterprises. Yet normally he will have no acumen for business, will employ political cronies instead of competent professionals, and will lack incentive to control his expenses because he can survive on money that he takes from others. Hence the cost that he incurs to produce a unit of a good will usually exceed not only the costs that other producers would incur to produce it, but also the price of the unit at equilibrium. His expenses will certainly exceed his revenues when he produces goods that no one would buy at any price in a free society, such as nuclear weapons and concentration camps.

Unlike people who subsist through voluntary exchange, a controller can continue to produce goods when his expenses exceed his revenues because he can subsidize his operations with stolen property; however, he will prefer to earn a profit. Therefore, he will usually arrogate unto himself a *monopoly* over the production of all goods of the kinds that he produces, thereby eliminating the supply of the goods of his competitors and raising the demand for his own goods. A monopoly also serves a greater purpose for the controller: it allows him to maintain control of his subjects more easily by reducing their abilities to resist his systemic violence. His monopolization of production of:

- water, food, medicine, shelter, and clothing will force a populace to depend upon him for survival;
- money will allow him to debase a currency in order to obtain goods without producing goods in exchange (see section 10.8);
- roads, bridges, and transportation will allow him to track and restrain movement of the populace;
- provisions for security (e.g., guns, guards, militia, technology for encryption) will render the populace defenseless against him;
- judicial services will allow him and his henchmen to use force under the sanction of a seemingly impartial court;
- conduits of information (e.g., television, radio, newspapers, social media) and communication (e.g., telephones, post, electronic mail) will allow him to disseminate propaganda and stifle the voices of his opponents;
- scholastic instruction will allow him to brainwash the populace and retard development of independent thought.

The members of a society will produce all the materials and services that they value sufficiently highly (including those of the kinds listed on the previous page) in adequate quantities in the absence of a controller because the signals of price and profit will direct them to produce goods with their limited resources in an assortment that will optimally meet their needs and wants (see section 6.3); indeed, only in a controlled society will people produce such goods in inadequate quantities. Nevertheless, when a controller monopolizes the production of goods of certain kinds for a long period of time, generations of people with no knowledge of economics or history can come to believe that they could not even survive without him.

In some sense, every person holds a natural monopoly over his own production because each individual supplies services in a unique way. Likewise, every company holds a natural monopoly over the unique good that it produces (see section 1.2). But monopolies over all goods of a certain kind cannot develop in a free society because restrictions on production require the initiation of violence. Only a controller can grant and enforce a privilege of such a monopoly, whether to himself or to others and whether in the form of a license, patent, or copyright.

10.8 Control and Debasement of Money

To acquire funds with which to enforce his will, placate his subjects, or live in luxury, a controller may take command over the production of the real money of society; however, high costs of production or short supplies of the monetary metal may prevent him from minting the money in a quantity sufficiently great to meet these ends adequately (see section 9.1). Hence a controller will often alter the composition of the money subsequent to his arrogation of its production by substituting a cheaper material for a dearer one. Indeed, as his control over the people of his territory expands to meet his ever growing lust for power, he must progressively debase the medium of exchange to increase the rate of its production.

Yet people will naturally reject an inferior money in favor of a superior one if available. Thus a controller must purge alternative tenders from the marketplace before he significantly debases his own. Should he proceed to debauch the medium of exchange to a material whereby he can create any amount of money at no extra cost, the lack of alternatives may then necessitate the continuance of its usage despite its inherent worthlessness. Nevertheless, ever rising rates of inflation will eventually drive the society toward a system of barter and impel the introduction of a new money (see section 8.4). While the controller will then promote for succession another money of costless material that he can produce without limit, the populace may resist and demand a metallic money or his deposition. In such case, he will accelerate his rate of production of the terminally depreciating currency and exchange it for as much gold and silver as he can before it fails completely.

11

Effects of Coercion

11.1 Distribution of Plunder

A controller will make enemies for himself as he exercises control over a territory. In order to preserve his life and maintain his control, he must use a portion of the money that he has stolen to hire protectors, enforcers, and agitators; however, he will establish control more securely when he can also convince a majority of the people living within the territory that the conditions under which they live are better (or less worse) than they would be in the absence of his interventions. Of course, some people truly will live better under his rule, most notably himself.

11.1.1 Welfare

A controller may give some of the money that he seizes to those toward whom many of the members of society feel compassion. By dispensing plunder to the poor, unemployed, sick, handicapped, feeble-minded, and elderly, he can gain political support not only from them, but also from those who mistake such non-sacrificial distributions of spoils for acts of generosity. *Welfare* of such forms will help financially all the people who receive it, though it can harm them psychologically if they grow dependent upon the controller.

11.1.2 Services

A controller can ingratiate himself to the public by directing most of the money that he steals toward services for commoners and seeming to skim only a modest wage for himself. With effective propaganda, he can usually earn goodwill by simply reporting the amounts of money that he has spent on such services regardless of their necessity or value. More importantly, he can ensure that a greater portion of the money eventually returns to him by channeling it through allies in exchange for future kickbacks or favors; however, to preserve the alliance the scheme must also enrich the providers of the services, who will invariably charge exorbitant fees for them.

11.1.3 Subsidies

A controller may disburse a portion of his plunder to sellers or buyers of goods in the form of *subsidies*. Any subsidy on a good will immediately cause the profit of its seller to rise. When given to the seller himself, it will cause his profit to rise directly by the amount of the subsidy. When given to buyers of the good, it will cause the profit of the seller to rise indirectly as it causes levels of demand for the good to rise and its price to reach equilibrium at a higher value.

Yet higher profits and yields will encourage producers and investors to direct more resources into production of a good (see section 5.2). Thus a subsidy also will cause levels of supply of the good to rise eventually and its price to reach equilibrium at a lower value. If the price of the good ultimately falls below its original level (as we may expect when the seller receives the subsidy), then the subsidy will help all buyers of the good. If the price remains above its original level (as we may expect when buyers receive the subsidy), then the subsidy will help only the buyers who receive it.

11.1.4 Foreign Aid

A controller may distribute booty to the controller of another territory in the name of *foreign aid* in order to exercise control over that region through him. Such gifts will alter the relationship between the puppet and the people of his territory. Normally a controller must maintain some interest in the welfare of his victims for the same reasons that a parasite must concern itself with the health of its host; for his own sake, he dare not impoverish or destroy them because he can regularly extract wealth from neither the indigent nor the dead. But a controller who periodically receives large amounts of money from a wealthier benefactor can terrorize the residents of his territory without repercussion. Indeed, he likely will find motivation to repress them in some way. If he wishes to eliminate threats to his power, wealth, and prestige, then he will confine (to prison or asylum), torture, starve, or annihilate members of the populace. If he wishes to improve the territorial body under a prideful delusion of divine omniscience, then he will indoctrinate, relocate, drug, or sterilize them. Of course, these forms of repression are not mutually exclusive.

11.1.5 Escalation of Need

Distributions of money will generate need for greater distributions. Disbursements to people out of work will promote unemployment, payments for medical services will encourage frequent visits to the doctor, subsidies on goods will stimulate greater production of the goods, foreign aid will more severely impoverish the people of a country, and so forth. Hence the total cost of such benevolence may well rise beyond the initial estimates of a controller. To reduce this cost, he must slash the size of his payments, constrict the number of their recipients, or depress the supply of the items under subsidization; however, he can do so only at the risk of antagonizing the plebeians.

11.2 The Black Market

Victims of oppression often try to evade controls in order to improve or extend their lives. The *black market* of a territory is the space in which its residents voluntarily exchange goods in violation of the commands of its controller. Many people who transact business in a black market eventually clash with a controller in some manner.

The price of a good in a black market will differ from its price in an authorized market in the direction of its price in a free market; however, the price in a black market will always exceed the price in a free market because effective restrictions on the sale, purchase, price, or production of a good will cause levels of supply of the good to fall. Rigid restrictions on sales can cause prices in a black market to rise to extremely high levels and allow producers who take the risk of providing goods to consumers therein to reap substantial rewards.

11.3 Consolidation in Industry

As taxes, ceilings, floors, restrictions, regulations, or other controls reduce their profits, marginally solvent producers will face liquidation. They must then either discontinue their operations or merge them with those of their competitors. Hence infringements on voluntary exchange will tend to diminish the number but enlarge the sizes of the businesses in a society. A controller will usually welcome (if not encourage) such consolidation because he can exercise control more easily over fewer large businesses than over many small ones.

Producers themselves can guide or accelerate processes of consolidation by enticing controllers to impose burdens that cripple their competitors. Directors of large businesses in particular will tend to promote tighter controls because producers with high revenues can tolerate greater regulation (see subsection 10.5.3) and pay greater *bribes* than producers with low revenues. In fact, the influence of directors of large banks and corporations on a controller can grow so strong that the former effectively usurp the power of the latter, although we cannot always demarcate the divisions of real command in a society between bankers, corporate administrators, and nominal controllers. The members of the true *ruling elite* of a territory often exercise control clandestinely through a series of interchangeable and disposable figureheads to prevent the commoners within their dominion from holding them to account for policies that spread misery.

11.4 Cooperation between Controllers and Bankers

Of all businessmen, bankers generally maintain the friendliest relationships with controllers because their interests most dependably coincide. A controller will normally want his subjects to patronize banks because he can confiscate funds and gather incriminating financial records more easily when they keep their money in a central repository and transfer it by cheque or by wire than when they spread it among countless hidden caches and pay for goods in cash. To encourage them to use a bank, he may insure the deposits therein against burglary, fire, or mismanagement, disseminate propaganda that exaggerate the ease or sophistication with which it can facilitate the transfer of money, or restrict the use of cash in transactions on the pretext that such enables criminal activity. But these actions will provide as much benefit to bankers as to the controller; the insurance will allow them to reap the gains from their activities without risk of loss, while the propaganda and restrictions on cash will stimulate greater sales of their services.

Both controllers and bankers will derive further benefit from the adoption by the populace of a money that the former can produce in arbitrarily high quantities without cost (see section 10.8). Such a costless money will enable a controller not only to purchase more units of goods, but also to reimburse and pacify depositors when banks fail. Thus it will allow bankers to produce substitutive money far in excess of the real money they hold, use the unrealizable money to purchase more units of goods themselves, and escape reprisal from swindled customers when their banks inevitably collapse (see subsection 7.3.6).

Yet people will not normally accept a costless money in exchange for goods (see section 9.1). Hence a controller can first establish a *pseudo* money only subtilely and gradually on the basis of a real money currently in use. In multiple stages over a long period of time, he will allow bankers to abrogate their obligations to redeem substitutive money, prohibit the circulation of tangible media of exchange, and force the members of society to execute their purchases and sales with transfers of funds through authorized banks. By the end of this period, the money of society will consist mostly of entries in ledgers of banks and the controller himself will produce the *de facto* real money of society with the stroke of a pen in a primary ledger (though for the sake of appearance he may delegate his authority over regulation of the pseudo money to a central bank ostensibly charged to operate for the good of the people). At this juncture, the controller may officially sever any link between the pseudo money and the original real money.

11.5 Fulfillment of Needs

To progress toward optimal fulfillment of their needs and wants, the members of society must produce for consumption goods of higher quality in greater quantity and variety (see sections 1.3 and 6.1) by directing their production and savings into goods and capital that maximize their profits and yields in response to prices that reflect their voluntary expenditures (see section 6.3).

But nearly all forms of violent action will inhibit such production, consumption, direction, maximization, or reflection. If a controller prohibits producers from selling goods, incapacitates producers through injury or imprisonment, murders producers, constrains procreation, discourages commercial activity by stealing revenues or profits, discourages labor by stealing or withholding wages, idles willing workers with an effective floor on wages, withholds land from productive use, or enables people to avoid productive activity with gifts of welfare, then he will reduce production. If he prohibits consumers from buying goods, steals the earnings or property of consumers, destroys goods that consumers have bought, or wastes goods through unprofitable production, then he will reduce consumption. If he imposes controls on rates of interest, steals the savings of potential investors, or discourages accumulation of plant by stealing or destroying property, then he will reduce investment in capital. If he compels people to produce certain goods or produces goods himself, then he will substitute his subjective whims for the objective incentives of profit. And if he subsidizes producers or consumers of goods, compels people to spend money on goods, spends money he steals on goods, or imposes controls on prices, then he will distort prices.

Therefore, most actions of a controller will ensure less adequate fulfillment of the needs and wants of the members of society. As he acts with greater frequency or intensity, his efforts will lead to greater deficiencies of goods.

11.6 Crisis

In the free market, natural limitations inhibit the creation of money at superoptimal rates (see sections 9.1 and 9.2) and forestall consequent inequities and destruction of wealth. But when a controller assumes command over the money of a society (see section 10.8), he effectively removes the safeguards that preclude such havoc; the costlessness of a fiat currency will allow him to produce excessive quantities of real money, while indemnity from losses will encourage bankers to produce greater quantities of unrealizable substitutive money (see section 11.4). Thus central control of money guarantees that a society must proceed through a cycle of economic expansion and contraction (see section 8.1).

Nevertheless, a controller will often try to perpetuate the phase of expansion and dodge the phase of contraction. He will typically believe that he can not only circumvent the unfavorable consequences of monetary deflation, but also sustain the favorable consequences of monetary inflation as long as he continues to produce his pseudo money in sufficient quantities. This simplistic response to a deflationary problem must ultimately lead to a greater inflationary crisis (see section 8.4).

11.7 Beneficial Coercion

People will attain maximum prosperity only when they can produce, consume, and trade freely because coercion will prevent them from fulfilling their needs and wants most adequately (see section 11.5). Nevertheless, *retributive* coercion will affect all nonviolent members of society beneficially by constraining or redressing the harm that malevolent actors cause. Execution of murderers and kidnappers will prevent them from murdering and kidnapping again, punitive seizure of the property of thieves will discourage them from stealing, like injury to injurers will discourage them from injuring, liberation of captives will allow them to engage in productive labor, and recovery of stolen property will restore the incentive of the victims to produce.

Generally then, punishment for acts of violence and recompense for damages will afford the members of society greater peace and allow them to maximize their production. Yet a person can harm himself even in the absence of coercion. Fornication, harlotry, sodomy, and bestiality will degrade him, adultery will destabilize his marriage and family, and assumption of unserviceable debt will enslave him. Behavior of these kinds can also grieve the innocent. Children of fornicators and harlots may never know their fathers, children or wives of adulterers and debtors may face separation from their fathers or husbands, and relatives of fornicators, harlots, and sodomites will suffer shame and the scorn of their neighbors.

If not checked, immorality will spread through a society as prurient peers, rapacious elites, blackmailers, and potential creditors exert ever greater pressure on the populace (particularly the young, ignorant, destitute, or otherwise vulnerable) to engage in such activity. Agents of malevolent powers will also exploit lawlessness in order to deliberately weaken the society, employing visual media to stimulate carnal impulses, false arguments to undermine the moral authority of parents, churches, and holy scriptures, and promises of material satisfaction to promote indebtedness. For absolute license will ultimately lead to brokenness and instability across a significant segment of a society, demoralize its members thoroughly, and threaten its very viability. Therefore, though they encroach upon liberties as forms of *initiative* coercion, effective prohibitions on fornication, harlotry, sodomy, bestiality, and adultery and periodic compulsory release from debt will also affect the members of society positively.

12

The Law

12.1 The Law

To maximize their health and prosperity, the members of a society must live by a law that limits acts of coercion to those necessary to preserve society itself (see sections 11.5 and 11.7). Mercifully, the LORD has given such a law to us.

12.1.1 Prohibitions on Violence and Immorality

The Law prohibits many forms of violence and immorality. In the commandments "thou shalt not kill" (Ex 20:13), "thou shalt not steal" (Ex 20:15), "thou shalt not commit adultery" (Ex 20:14), and "thou shalt not bear false witness against thy neighbor" (Ex 20:16), the Law explicitly prohibits destruction of person or property (see section 10.2), seizure of person or property (see section 10.3), licentious activity (see section 11.7), and false witness that perverts justice. In the instruction of Moses that "ye shall not add unto the word which I command you, neither shall ye diminish aught from it" (Deut 4:2), the Law also implicitly prohibits controls on prices (see section 10.4), controls on exchanges (see section 10.5), claims to unused land (see section 10.6), monopolies over production (see section 10.7), controls on money (see section 10.8), and restrictions on procreation.

12.1.2   Enforcement of Prohibitions

The Law mandates the use of coercion to discourage, constrain, and redress violence and immorality. The appropriate punishment for:

- murder is death (see Lev 24:17);
- kidnapping is death (see Deut 24:7);
- theft, fraud, vandalism, and arson is compensation to the victim (see Lev 24:18,21), possibly to a multiple of the value of the object stolen, defaced, or destroyed (see Ex 22:1,4);
- injury is like injury to the injurer (see Lev 24:19–20);
- fornication with a virgin is a monetary fine and compulsory marriage (see Ex 22:16, Deut 22:28–29);
- concealment of fornication under a pretense of virginity is death (see Deut 22:13–14,20–21);
- harlotry by a national is death (see Deut 22:20–21, 23:17);
- sodomy is death (see Lev 20:13, Deut 23:17);
- bestiality is death (see Lev 20:15-16);
- adultery is death (see Lev 20:10);
- false witness is the punishment that the witness thought to have done to the accused (see Deut 19:16–19)

The Law does not sanction the use of prisons or torture in the administration of justice.

12.1.3   Positive Commands

The Law includes positive commands that people should obey to their benefit. Obedience to the command "be fruitful, and multiply, and replenish the earth, and subdue it: and have dominion over the fish of the sea, and over the fowl of the air, and over every living thing that moveth upon the earth" (Gen 1:28) will enable the members of society to meet their needs and wants as consumers more adequately through narrower division of labor and production of a greater quantity or variety of goods (see section 5.6).

Obedience to the command "thou shalt have a perfect and just weight, a perfect and just measure shalt thou have" (Deut 25:15) will preclude the discouragement of production or consumption that surreptitious theft would cause (see section 11.5) and the destructive cycle of economic expansion and contraction (see section 8.1) that a debasement of the medium of exchange would initiate (see section 10.8). And obedience to the command "at the end of every seven years thou shalt make a release" from debt where "every creditor that lendeth ought unto his neighbor shall release it" (Deut 15:1–3) will cleanse the society of liabilities, liberate debtor from creditor, and provide incentive for the former slave (see Prov 22:7) to engage in greater production by allowing him to keep all that he earns.

On the other hand, constraints on procreation, prevention of the cultivation, development, or occupation of wilderness, elevation of beast to the level of man (or depression of man to the level of beast), debasement of money, fraud, and permanent enslavement of debtors will discourage production or consumption and reduce the quantities and varieties of goods available to the members of society (see section 11.5). Therefore, actions or edicts of men that violate or prevent execution of the positive commands of God will lead to economic decline.

12.2 Guidelines for Governance

The LORD has also provided us with a political model in the nation of Israel.

12.2.1 Division of the Nation

The nation of Israel functioned as a union of distinct tribes. Though all men of Israel lived under the same Law, each received justice executed within his tribe (see Deut 16:18), inherited land within the lot that fell to his tribe (see Jos 15:1–19:48), and fought under the standard (see Num 10:14–27;

Jdg 1:3, 12:1), served under the ruler (see 1Chr 27:16–22), and spoke in the dialect of his tribe (see Jdg 12:5–6). Perpetuation of the tribal division of Israel would later serve to confine apostasy to a single tribe and forestall the eradication of the entire nation (see Jdg 19:1–21:25).

At the time the Israelites first approached the land of Canaan to take occupation, the men of the twelve tribes (excluding Levi) numbered 603,550 in total and 50,295 per tribe on average, with 32,200 men in the smallest tribe and 74,600 men in the largest (see Num 1:17–46). Though they failed to take the land at this time, they prepared again to enter Canaan after a journey of forty years in the wilderness that purged them of disobedience. The men of Israel then numbered 601,730 in total and 50,145 per tribe on average, with 22,200 men in the smallest tribe and 76,500 men in the largest (see Num 26:1–51). The consistency in the sizes of the populations 40 years apart suggests that the ideal number of men in a tribe lay roughly between 25,000 and 75,000 with an average of 50,000.

12.2.2 Territory of the Tribes

The size of the territory that the tribes of Israel were to divide and occupy was roughly 12,000 square miles. Hence the land would support about 50 men of Israel (excluding the Levites) per square mile on average. If we assume that the ratio of the number of males "from a month old and upward" to the number of males "from thirty years old and upward even unto fifty years old" was the same for all Israel as for the Levites and that the number of males of Israel between thirty years old to fifty years old was half the number "from twenty years old and upward" (since all males over sixty years old would have been laid low during the journey of forty years; see Num 26:64), then the males of Israel from a month old and upward would have numbered roughly 770,000 (equal to $(601{,}730 \div 2) \times (22{,}000 \div 8{,}580)$) at the time they entered Canaan (see Num 3:39, 4:46–48).

If we further assume that the number of females of Israel was equal to the number of males, then the people of Israel would have numbered roughly 1,540,000 in total. Thus the land might have supported roughly 130 people of Israel (excluding the Levites) per square mile on average. Since Levites, foreigners, and slaves would also live in the land, the population density therein may have fallen between 150 and 200 people per square mile.

Joshua gave smaller families a smaller lot and larger families a larger one (see Num 26:54, 33:54), but he directed the members of a tribe that was too large for its lot to expand into a wood to which the Canaanites had laid claim (see Jos 17:14–18). Indeed, God had commanded the Israelites to displace the savage nations who had arrogated the land unto themselves (see Num 33:50–53), though little by little so that the wild beasts would not increase upon them (see Deut 7:22). The mandate to fill the land forbade the Israelites from confining themselves to a small subdivision of their territory and allowing the density of the population within it to rise ever higher.

12.2.3 Selection of Rulers

On the advice of his father-in-law (see Ex 18:12–27), Moses charged the Israelites to take "wise men, and understanding, known among your tribes, and I will make them rulers over you" (Deut 1:13). Of "able men, such as fear God, men of truth, hating covetousness", he would make "rulers of thousands, rulers of hundreds, rulers of fifties, and rulers of tens" that "at all seasons" could judge "righteously between every man and his brother, and the stranger that is with him" according to the "ordinances and laws" of God (see Ex 18:20–25; Deut 1:16). Presumably, the rulers of tens would judge the smallest matters, the rulers of fifties larger matters, the rulers of hundreds larger matters still, the rulers of thousands even larger matters, and Moses himself the largest matters (see Ex 18:26).

A man could have justifiably promoted someone for the office of ruler only if he knew him to be wise, but he would likely have known only kinsmen or neighbors well enough to assess their characters. Thus we may surmise that the men of each tribe divided into groups of ten from the same family or neighborhood and that the ten men in each group then chose one of themselves to rule over them. All such rulers of ten could have then divided similarly into groups of five from the same extended family or region, where the five rulers of ten in each group would choose one of themselves to rule over the fifty. Rulers of the same rank could have then continued to divide into groups of five in the same way, where five rulers of fifties would choose a ruler of hundreds (250), five rulers of hundreds would choose a ruler of thousands (1250), five rulers of thousands would choose a ruler of a greater number of thousands (6250), and the five rulers of the greater number of thousands would choose the head of the tribe.

This mechanism of selection of rulers would have perfectly served a tribe of 31,250 men, but it would have perfectly served a tribe of 77,600 men if six rulers would have chosen a ruler of the next higher rank instead of five. Since the sizes of all of the tribes of Israel except Simeon fell between 31,250 and 77,600 men at the time of their entry into Canaan, we may conclude that a process in which either five or six rulers of a given rank would select a ruler of rank immediately above theirs would have served almost every tribe well.

12.2.4 Membership in the Assembly

Presentation of the chiefs of Israel before the assembly of the people of God (see Jdg 20:2) suggests that members of the assembly held responsibility for the selection of rulers. Yet the assembly was not open to every man, woman, and child who lived in the land. The Law not only restricted membership in the congregation of the LORD to males of

Israel "from twenty years old and upward" (Num 1:2–3), but also denied entrance into the congregation to him who "is wounded in the stones, or hath his privy member cut off", to the "bastard" and his descendants to the tenth generation, to the Ammonite and Moabite and their descendants forever, and to the Edomite and Egyptian and their descendants to the third generation (see Deut 23:1–8). Thus descendants of foreigners closely related to the Israelites or hospitable to them could eventually join the congregation after a period of time lengthy enough to ensure their obedience to the Law and their assimilation into the nation, but descendants of foreigners hostile to Israel could never join the congregation.

12.2.5   Administration of the State

Political guidelines for the nation of Israel dictate that the people and regions of the world divide into distinct states to contain the spread of disobedience and apostasy. These autonomous states should accommodate a citizenry numbering between 25,000 and 75,000 men, plus women and children. A state with more than 75,000 men should divide into smaller states. If the density of population in a particular state should come to significantly exceed 50 men of the assembly per square mile, then a portion of that population should migrate to unoccupied territory and bring the land there under cultivation or development.

The people of a state must restrict membership in its assembly to men of age twenty years and upward who were born in wedlock, whose ancestors to ten generations were born in wedlock, and whose private parts remain whole. They must also deny foreigners any right to rule or to participate in the process of selection of rulers. They may allow the grandsons of foreigners who take residence in the state to join the political body, but only if they hail from states with denizens hospitable to themselves. The descendants of foreigners hostile to the nation must never be allowed to join the assembly.

Small subsets of members of the assembly must choose wise men who fear God (see Prov 9:10) and know His ordinances and laws to rule over themselves at the local level. These local rulers should settle all small matters of dispute, but they should choose rulers at higher levels of authority to adjudicate more difficult matters. Rulers must serve as judges who rightly interpret and enforce the eternal Law of God in light of the teachings of Jesus Christ and revelations of the Holy Spirit, not as legislators who create their own law.

12.3 Conclusion

For health and prosperity, we need no economists to inform us, central planners to guide us, or controllers to violate us; we need only to learn and obey the eternal law of the LORD (see Deut 7:12–15; 1Chr 22:13; Matt 5:18).

PART III

Examples

13

Examples for Part I

Example 1
Human beings act as individuals.

A. The statement "the family ate dinner" means that each individual in the family (father, mother, son, etc.) ate food, not that a single organism called a "family" with a mouth and stomach did so.

B. The statement "England declares war on France" means that certain individuals in the English government declare their hostility toward certain individuals in the French government (or toward people living in the territory ruled by them), not that a single organism called "England" will fight a single organism called "France."

C. The statement "Smith Construction, Incorporated, built the house" means that certain individuals who worked for the company performed tasks such as mixing cement, laying a foundation, erecting a frame, shingling a roof, and installing windows, not that a single organism performed all these tasks.

D. The statement "Team X defeated Team Y in the baseball game" means that the individuals on Team X crossed home plate more times than did the individuals on Team Y, not that single organisms called "teams" ever crossed home plate.

Example 2
A person can allocate his time and resources toward only a finite number of ends.

A. A boy can go to the stadium or to the theater at 7:00 PM this evening, but he cannot go to both of these places at the same time.

B. A woman can use a cup of water to quench her thirst, wash her face, or irrigate her garden, but she cannot use the entire cup on all these tasks.

C. A man can use a specific unit of steel to make the body of a car, a piece of cutlery, or a girder for a bridge, but he cannot use it in all three items.

Example 3
Human beings use goods to achieve ends.

A. People use bread to satisfy their need for food.

B. People use television sets to satisfy their desire for entertainment.

C. People use lessons on a piano to satisfy their desire to learn how to play the piano.

Example 4
Every exchangeable good is either tangible (a material) or intangible (a service).

A. Loaves of bread, wine glasses, television sets, computers, pieces of furniture, toothbrushes, mops, and automobiles are materials.

B. Lessons on a piano, labor to repair a bicycle, and professional athletic performances are services.

Example 5
The values that people place on units of goods may change.

A. If the temperature of the air rises, then the value that a man places on a heavy coat may fall.

B. If a manufacturer promotes shovels of a certain kind, then the value that a gardener places on a shovel of that kind may rise.

C. If all of her friends begin to wear dresses when outside of the home, then the value that a woman places on a pair of pants may fall.

D. If medical "experts" assert that the consumption of grapes prevents cancer, then the value that a person with faith in experts places on a cluster of grapes may rise.

E. A person may prefer a sandwich with ham over a sandwich with chicken one day, but prefer the latter over the former the next day.

F. A person may prefer $100 over a hour of leisure when young and poor, but prefer the time of leisure over the money when old and rich.

Example 6
People produce tangible goods by mixing their labor with ingredients by means of plant.

A. A baker produces bread by mixing his labor with flour, oil, salt, yeast, water, and heat by means of a mixer and an oven.

B. A driver who transports milk from a dairy to a grocery store produces the good "milk-at-store" by mixing his labor with the ingredient "milk-at-dairy" by means of a truck.

Example 7
Products that differ in substance, size, shape, location, condition, grade, or any other quality are different goods.

A. A car and a banana are units of different goods.

B. A car produced by automaker X and a car produced by automaker Y are units of different goods.

C. A small car made by automaker X and a large car made by automaker X are units of different goods.

D. A new car at a local dealership and a new car of the same make and model at a distant dealership are units of different goods.

E. Two used cars of the same make and model are units of different goods.

F. Two unmarked bars of pure copper that have the same size and shape and lie in the same location are units of the same good, even if different refiners produced the bars.

Example 8
Different people place different values on goods.

A. Given three hours of leisure time, one boy may prefer to watch a movie while another boy may prefer to watch a game of baseball.

B. Given a cup of water, one girl may use it to quench her thirst, another may use it to wash her hair, while yet another may use it to irrigate her garden.

C. Given a choice between a hamburger and a slice of pizza, one person may prefer the hamburger while another may prefer the pizza.

Example 9
Two people will trade units of goods voluntarily if and only if each of them places a higher value on the unit that the other person possesses than on the unit that he himself possesses.

A. If Farmer A owns a goat and Farmer B owns five chickens, then the farmers will not exchange the rights of ownership to these animals unless A would prefer the five chickens over his goat and B would prefer the goat over his five chickens.

B. Barber X will not cut the hair of Gentleman Y for ten units of money unless X would prefer ten units of money over fifteen minutes of leisure and Y would prefer a haircut from X over ten units of money in his possession.

Example 10
The interval of prices at which a person would buy a unit of a good that he wants will have some upper limit and the interval of prices at which he would sell a unit of a good that he owns will have some lower limit.

A. A person might buy a pound of cheese for $6 or less, but not for more than $6.

B. A person might sell his couch for $250 or more, but not for less than $250.

Example 11
We cannot combine meaningfully quantities of disparate goods.

A. We cannot add together five dogs and three cats to obtain eight dog-cats.

B. We cannot add together ten bushels of flour at store S_1 and seven bushels of flour at store S_2 to obtain seventeen bushels of flour at store S_1-and-S_2.

Example 12
The values at which the prices of different goods reach equilibrium will usually differ.

A. We should not expect all workers to earn the same wage.

B. We should not expect a bushel of flour at store X to cost the same amount of money as a bushel of flour at store Y.

C. We should not expect the price of a damaged radio to equal the price of an undamaged radio of the same kind.

Example 13
- *The demand for a good at a lower price will be greater than or equal to the demand for the good at a higher price.*
- *The supply of a good at a lower price will be less than or equal to the supply of the good at a higher price.*
- *To avoid a surplus or shortage, a seller must adjust the price of his good downward from values at which a surplus exists and upward from values at which a shortage exists.*
- *The graphs of the equations $q = s(p)$ and $q = d(p)$ will intersect at the point with coordinates (p_e, q_e), where p_e is the value at which the price of a good would reach equilibrium and q_e is the quantity of the good that buyers and sellers would exchange at that price.*

Suppose buyers B_1, B_2, B_3, B_4, and B_5 visit a merchant to purchase lampstands. Table 1 shows the maximum number of ounces of silver that each buyer would pay for a lampstand. Table 2 shows the minimum number of ounces of silver that the merchant would accept in exchange for a lampstand. Let us assume that the lampstands that the merchant sells are identical, that neither the buyers nor the seller prefer one lampstand over another, and that each buyer wants to purchase only one lampstand.

From these tables we can generate formulas for supply and demand (see Formulas 1 and 2) and from these for-

Buyer	Maximum Price
B_1	100
B_2	110
B_3	120
B_4	130
B_5	140

Table 1: Maximum Prices of Buyers of Lampstands

Lampstand	Minimum Price
First	100
Second	110
Third	120
Fourth	130
Fifth	140

Table 2: Minimum Prices of the Seller of Lampstands

$$d(p) = \begin{cases} 5 & \text{if } \ \ 0 \leq p \leq 100 \\ 4 & \text{if } 100 < p \leq 110 \\ 3 & \text{if } 110 < p \leq 120 \\ 2 & \text{if } 120 < p \leq 130 \\ 1 & \text{if } 130 < p \leq 140 \\ 0 & \text{if } 140 < p \end{cases}$$

Formula 1: Demand for Lampstands

$$s(p) = \begin{cases} 0 & \text{if } \ \ 0 \leq p < 100 \\ 1 & \text{if } 100 \leq p < 110 \\ 2 & \text{if } 110 \leq p < 120 \\ 3 & \text{if } 120 \leq p < 130 \\ 4 & \text{if } 130 \leq p < 140 \\ 5 & \text{if } 140 \leq p \end{cases}$$

Formula 2: Supply of Lampstands

mulas we can generate graphs of supply and demand (see Figure 5). Since the graphs intersect at the point $(120, 3)$, the price of the lampstands will reach equilibrium at 120 oz and the quantity of lampstands that the merchant would sell at this price is three (to buyers B_3, B_4, and B_5). Were the merchant to set his price to 120 oz and complete these sales, he would not transact business with buyers B_1 and B_2 because the minimum prices that he would require in exchange for the remaining two (i.e., the fourth and the fifth) lampstands that he would own would exceed the maximum prices that they would pay for them.

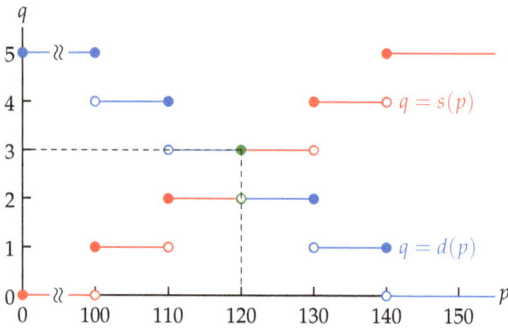

Figure 5: Graphs of Supply and Demand for Lampstands

Figure 5 also reveals the imbalances in supply and demand at all prices other than 120 oz and justifies the tendencies toward equilibrium. At a price above 120 oz, a surplus of lampstands will exist because the supply will exceed the demand there. Though the merchant may initially try to sell, for example, four lampstands at a price of 135 oz apiece, he will find only one willing buyer (namely B_5). Yet he will likely discover that he can sell another lampstand (to B_4) if he lowers his price to, say, 125 oz, and then finally a third lampstand (to B_3) if he lowers his price again to 120 oz.

On the other hand, a shortage will exist at a price below

120 oz because the demand will exceed the supply there. The seller may initially try to sell, for example, one lampstand at a price of 105 oz, but he will find four willing buyers (namely B_2, B_3, B_4, or B_5). Encouraged by his ability to sell a first lampstand quickly, he will discover that he can sell a second lampstand even if he raises his price to 115 oz, and still a third lampstand if he raises his price again to 120 oz. He may be able to sell the third lampstand at an even higher price, depending on which buyers purchased the first two.

Buyers do not usually enter the market for a good at the same time or remain in the market forever. So while a seller could earn more profit in some cases by initially setting the price of his good above that at equilibrium and then gradually lowering it, he would also run the risk of failing to sell units to early potential buyers who will not purchase units at a higher price but would have purchased units at the lower price at equilibrium. He might also earn more profit by initially setting the price of his good below that at equilibrium and then gradually raising it, but here he would run the risk of selling units at a lower price to buyers who would have purchased the good at the higher price at equilibrium.

Example 14
Schedules of supply and demand will determine for every good (both materials and services) the value at which its price reaches equilibrium.

Suppose the owner of company XYZ decides to hire a bookkeeper. After soliciting and reviewing applications for the position, he interviews three candidates: Alex, Bill, and Carl. He then decides that he will pay up to:

- ¥210000 per month for the services of Bill
- ¥200000 per month for the services of Alex
- ¥190000 per month for the services of Carl

Meanwhile, the three finalists have evaluated the position with respect to the expectations of the owner, the environment in which they would work, alternative prospects they may have, and other considerations. Each has determined the minimum salary he is willing to accept in exchange for his services at XYZ:

- Bill will not take the job for less than ¥220000 per month
- Alex will not take the job for less than ¥190000 per month
- Carl will not take the job for less than ¥160000 per month

The owner offers the job to Bill first. Figure 6 shows the graphs of supply and demand for the good "Bookkeeping Services performed at XYZ by Bill" at the time of the offer. Since these graphs do not intersect (or rather, they intersect where $q = 0$), no exchange can take place; Bill will reject the terms of the owner and refuse the position.

The owner offers the job to Alex next. Figure 7 shows

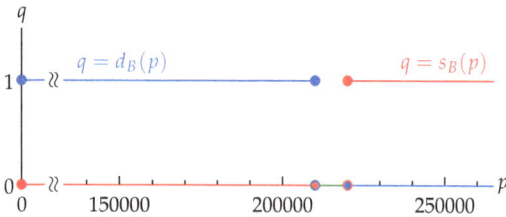

Figure 6: Graphs of Supply and Demand for Services of Bill

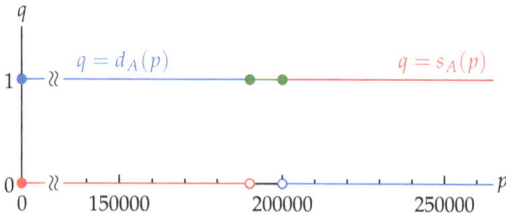

Figure 7: Graphs of Supply and Demand for Services of Alex

the graphs of supply and demand for the good "Bookkeeping Services performed at XYZ by Alex" at the time of this second offer. These graphs intersect at points (p, q) where $p \in [190000, 200000]$ and $q = 1$. Hence Alex will accept the position at some salary between ¥190000 and ¥200000 per month. The owner now concludes the process of filling the position and will not demand the services of Carl at any point in time.

Example 15
- *Points on a graph of supply will often align horizontally.*
- *The price of a good may reach equilibrium at all values within some interval.*
- *If the demand for a good rises at a price that had reached equilibrium, then supply will now equal demand at a higher price.*

The owner of a small restaurant sells three hamburgers by auction at noon each day. On one particular day, five customers bid on the hamburgers. The second column of Table 3 shows the maximum price that each will pay for a hamburger on this day, Formula 3 shows the corresponding schedule of demand for the hamburgers, and Figure 8 shows the graphs of supply and demand for the hamburgers with monetary amounts denominated in grams of silver. As the points of intersection of the graphs indicate, the price will reach equilibrium this day at some value in the interval $(4.5, 5.2]$.

| | Maximum Price | |
Customer	Day 1	Day 2
C_1	3.8	3.8
C_2	4.5	6.3
C_3	5.2	5.2
C_4	5.9	5.9
C_5	6.6	6.6

Table 3: Maximum Prices of Customers of Hamburgers

$$d_1(p) = \begin{cases} 5 & \text{if } 0 \le p \le 3.8 \\ 4 & \text{if } 3.8 < p \le 4.5 \\ 3 & \text{if } 4.5 < p \le 5.2 \\ 2 & \text{if } 5.2 < p \le 5.9 \\ 1 & \text{if } 5.9 < p \le 6.6 \\ 0 & \text{if } 6.6 < p \end{cases}$$

Formula 3: Demand for Hamburgers on Day 1

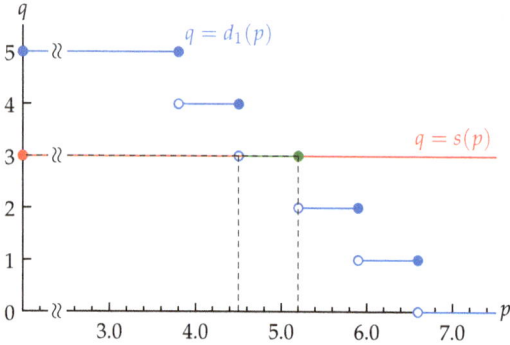

Figure 8: Graphs of Supply and Demand on Day 1

Now suppose that the same five customers also bid on the hamburgers the next day, but this time customer C_2 will pay up to 6.3 grams for a hamburger (see the third column of Table 3). Formula 4 and Figure 9 show the schedule of demand and the graphs of supply and demand for the hamburgers that result. Observe that the demand for the hamburgers has increased by one unit at each price in the interval $(4.5, 6.3]$ and that the price will reach equilibrium now at any value in the interval $(5.2, 5.9]$.

Note that the the bounds of the interval on which the price of the hamburgers will reach equilibrium would not have changed in every situation where demand increased between Day 1 and Day 2. For example, the bounds would have remained the same if the maximum price that C_5 was willing to pay rose to 7.1 grams because the price that he was willing to pay the previous day (namely 6.6 grams) was

$$d_2(p) = \begin{cases} 5 & \text{if } \ 0 \leq p \leq 3.8 \\ 4 & \text{if } 3.8 < p \leq 5.2 \\ 3 & \text{if } 5.2 < p \leq 5.9 \\ 2 & \text{if } 5.9 < p \leq 6.3 \\ 1 & \text{if } 6.3 < p \leq 6.6 \\ 0 & \text{if } 6.6 < p \end{cases}$$

Formula 4: Demand for Hamburgers on Day 2

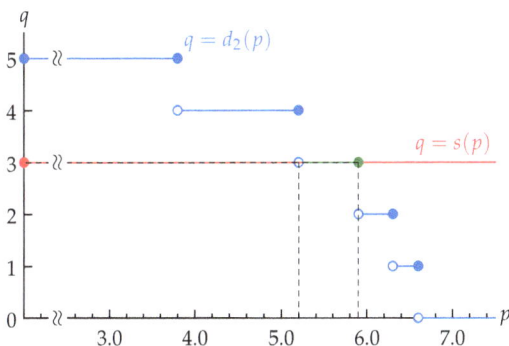

Figure 9: Graphs of Supply and Demand on Day 2

already above the highest price in the interval. The bounds would also have remained the same if the maximum price that C_1 was willing to pay rose to 4.2 grams because that price would still lie below the lowest price in the interval.

Example 16

○ *The demand for a good at any given price will generally be greater over a longer period of time than over a shorter period of time.*

○ *The value at which the price of a good would reach equilibrium will generally be higher over a longer period of time than over a shorter period of time if levels of supply of the good are the same over both periods.*

Suppose a shoemaker has made sixty pairs of shoes and wishes to sell them all within a certain period of time. Then the equation $s(p) = 60$ will define s, the function that returns the supply of the shoes over this period.

Further suppose that the demand for the shoes at any given price is the same on each day and that Formula 5 (with prices in ounces of copper) defines the function that returns the daily demand for the shoes. The demand for the shoes at a price p over an period of n days must therefore equal $n \cdot d_1(p)$. Hence Formulas 6, 7, and 8 will define the functions that return the demand for the shoes over periods of twelve, twenty, and sixty days.

By drawing the graph of s over the graphs of d_{12}, d_{20}, and d_{60} (see Figures 10, 11, and 12), we can determine for these periods the prices at which the shoemaker can sell his entire inventory (i.e., the prices at which supply does not exceed demand). Observe that he can sell all of the pairs of shoes:

- over 12 days if he sets the price per pair to 490 oz or less
- over 20 days if he sets the price per pair to 560 oz or less
- over 60 days if he sets the price per pair to 630 oz or less

In general then, the shoemaker can set a higher price on his product if he can wait longer for customers to exhaust his inventory; however, he will never sell any shoes if he sets the price above 630 ounces.

Example 17
Levels of demand for a good change when the ability of people to buy units of it change.

Immediately after Danny wins the lottery, the upper limits on the amounts of money that he is willing to spend rise for all kinds of food that he prefers at the local grocery store except grape jelly. Instead of grape jelly, he now chooses to spread caviar on his sandwiches. Thus the demand for the grape jelly at the grocery store will fall on some prices, but the demand for all other kinds of food at the grocery store that Danny prefers will rise on some prices.

$$d_1(p) = \begin{cases} 5 & \text{if} \quad 0 \le p \le 490 \\ 4 & \text{if} \quad 490 < p \le 525 \\ 3 & \text{if} \quad 525 < p \le 560 \\ 2 & \text{if} \quad 560 < p \le 595 \\ 1 & \text{if} \quad 595 < p \le 630 \\ 0 & \text{if} \quad 630 < p \end{cases}$$

Formula 5: Demand for Shoes Each Day

$$d_{12}(p) = \begin{cases} 60 & \text{if} \quad 0 \le p \le 490 \\ 48 & \text{if} \quad 490 < p \le 525 \\ 36 & \text{if} \quad 525 < p \le 560 \\ 24 & \text{if} \quad 560 < p \le 595 \\ 12 & \text{if} \quad 595 < p \le 630 \\ 0 & \text{if} \quad 630 < p \end{cases}$$

Formula 6: Demand for Shoes over Twelve Days

$$d_{20}(p) = \begin{cases} 100 & \text{if} \quad 0 \le p \le 490 \\ 80 & \text{if} \quad 490 < p \le 525 \\ 60 & \text{if} \quad 525 < p \le 560 \\ 40 & \text{if} \quad 560 < p \le 595 \\ 20 & \text{if} \quad 595 < p \le 630 \\ 0 & \text{if} \quad 630 < p \end{cases}$$

Formula 7: Demand for Shoes over Twenty Days

$$d_{60}(p) = \begin{cases} 300 & \text{if} \quad 0 \le p \le 490 \\ 240 & \text{if} \quad 490 < p \le 525 \\ 180 & \text{if} \quad 525 < p \le 560 \\ 120 & \text{if} \quad 560 < p \le 595 \\ 60 & \text{if} \quad 595 < p \le 630 \\ 0 & \text{if} \quad 630 < p \end{cases}$$

Formula 8: Demand for Shoes over Sixty Days

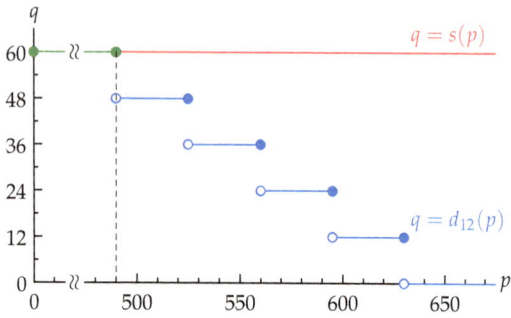

Figure 10: Graphs of Supply and Demand over Twelve Days

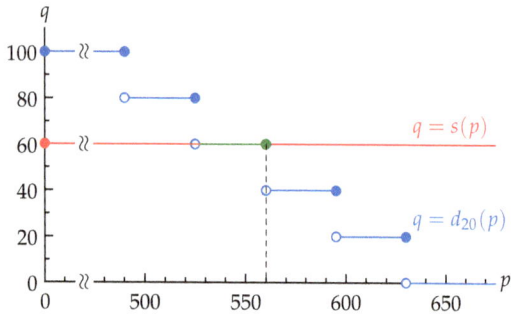

Figure 11: Graphs of Supply and Demand over Twenty Days

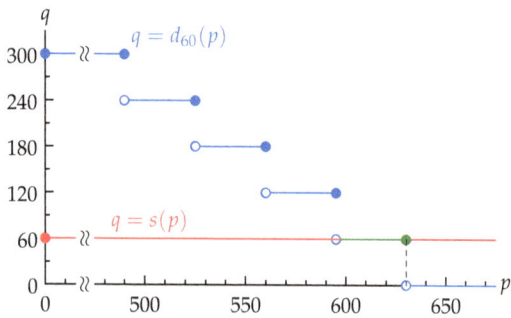

Figure 12: Graphs of Supply and Demand over Sixty Days

114

Example 18
Levels of demand for a good change when the willingness of people to buy units of it change.

Each day Dale visits a certain tavern to drink a certain kind of beer. He will pay up to $7.00 for a first pint, $4.75 for a second pint, and $1.50 for a third pint, but will not buy a fourth pint at any price. We denote his daily demand by d_1 and draw its graph in Figure 13.

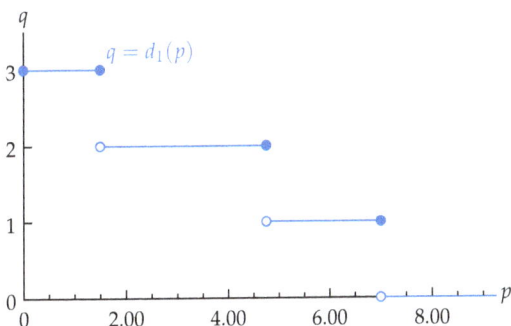

Figure 13: Demand of Dale for Beer before Assertion

Now suppose that Dale hears a trusted friend mention that consumption of beer causes flatulence. Disgusted, he loses some thirst for the beer. He remains willing to pay up to $5.50 for a first pint and $3.00 for a second pint of the beer, but he refuses to buy a third pint at any price. We denote his daily demand now by d_2 and draw its graph in Figure 14.

Dale's daily demand for the beer has decreased by one pint at every price on the intervals $[0, 1.50]$, $(3.00, 4.75]$, and $(5.50, 7.00]$. Therefore, the total demand for the beer from all members of society has also decreased to that extent at every price on those intervals, assuming that the demand from everyone other than Dale has remained the same at all prices.

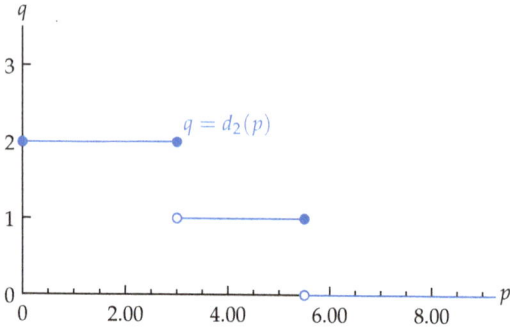

Figure 14: Demand of Dale for Beer after Assertion

Example 19

○ *Levels of supply of a good change when the ability of people to sell units of it change.*

○ *When a person produces a good at a higher rate, the supply of the good will rise from period to period.*

Theo bakes 500 donuts each day in his shop and must sell them all before they become stale the next day. While on a vacation, he realizes that he wants more money and determines to raise his rate of production to 800 donuts per day when he comes back to the shop. Upon his return, the daily supply of his donuts will rise by 300 units on all prices.

Example 20

Levels of supply of a good change when the willingness of people to sell units of it change.

Mabel places an advertisement in a newspaper to sell her antique vanity for $200. Her sister Nellie sees the advertisement and chides her for her willingness to sell the heirloom so cheaply. After some reflection, Mabel changes the price of the vanity to $225. Her decision has caused the supply of this unique piece of furniture to fall by one unit (from one unit to zero units) on the interval of prices $[200, 225)$.

Example 21

○ *Changes in levels of price can lead indirectly to changes in levels of demand.*

○ *If the seller of a good X raises its price and the increase causes a surplus, then the demand for other goods (especially those that serve the same purpose as X) should rise on some prices.*

Each week at a certain store, Edna buys one bar of soap of either brand X or brand Y. The prices for both brands are the same: 50 cents per bar. Edna prefers the soap of brand X for its richer lather, but she would buy the soap of brand Y if its price lay at least 5 cents below the price of the soap of brand X. At present then, her demand each week for the soap of brand X will equal one bar at every price less than 55 cents and zero bars at every price greater than or equal to 55 cents, while her demand each week for the soap of brand Y will be one bar at every price less than or equal to 45 cents and zero bars at every price greater than 45 cents (see Figure 15).

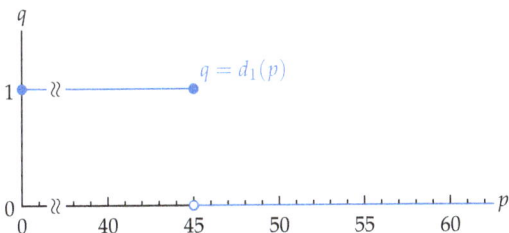

Figure 15: Demand of Edna for Soap of Brand Y before
Rise in Price of Soap of Brand X

Now suppose that the producer of the soap of brand X raises the price of his soap to 60 cents per bar. As a result, Edna will now purchase the soap of brand Y. Her demand each week for the soap of brand X will remain the same at every price, but her demand each week for the soap of brand Y will now equal one bar at every price less than or equal to 55 cents and zero bars at every price greater than 55 cents (see Figure 16).

Since Edna's weekly demand for the soap of brand Y has increased by one bar at prices on the interval $(45, 55]$, the weekly demand of all members of society for the soap of brand Y will also have increased to the same extent on the same interval if the levels of demand of everyone else have remained the same at all prices.

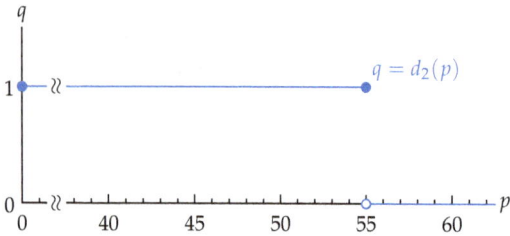

Figure 16: Demand of Edna for Soap of Brand Y after Rise in Price of Soap of Brand X

Example 22

○ *Changes in levels of supply can lead indirectly to changes in levels of demand.*

○ *If the supply of a good X rises at its current price to eliminate a shortage, then some people will now purchase more units of X. The demand for other goods (especially those that serve the same purpose as X) that these people prefer should then fall on some prices, though the demand for goods that they would use only in combination with X should rise on some prices.*

Suppose a producer raises his rate of production of tennis rackets to eliminate a national shortage at a certain price. As the supply of tennis rackets rises to meet the demand, people will buy more of them at that price. The demand for tennis balls should then also rise on some prices, but the demand for shuttlecocks may fall on some prices because people can play only one sport at a time.

Example 23

○ *Changes in levels of demand can lead indirectly to changes in other levels of demand.*

○ *If the demand for a good X rises at its current price and the seller of X fails to adjust that price in response, then no indirect changes in levels of demand will occur.*

A chef can sell 50 omelettes each morning for 20 francs apiece. Over time, his reputation grows and the daily demand for his omelettes rises from 50 to 75, but the chef refuses to raise their price. He will then continue to sell 50 omelettes each morning for 20 francs apiece and the increase in demand for them will not affect the demand for other goods.

Example 24

○ *Changes in levels of demand can lead indirectly to changes in levels of supply.*

○ *If the demand for a good falls at its current price and its producer fails to lower that price to eliminate or alleviate a surplus that results, then he will earn less revenue and profit on the sale of a lesser number of units of the good. Such decreases in profit will lead to lower rates of production and levels of supply of the good.*

Gary offers vegetarian dishes to customers at his restaurant. One day people realize that a diet with no meat has made them weak and easy to manipulate. Subsequently, many of his customers refuse to patronize the restaurant further. After a month of sluggish sales, Gary decides to close his business. This decision causes the supply of vegetarian dishes at his restaurant to fall to zero.

Example 25

○ *Changes in levels of supply can lead indirectly to changes in other levels of supply.*

○ *If levels of supply of ingredients, plant, or labor required for the production of a good change at their current prices and the producers of the ingredients adjust those prices to eliminate the shortages or surpluses that result, then the expenses of the producer of the good will also change. Lower expenses will mean higher profits while higher expenses will mean lower profits.*

Marilyn bakes and sells apple pies. One year, ideal weather allows the growers of apples to harvest a bumper crop. The increases in levels of supply of apples then cause the prices of apples to reach equilibrium at lower values. As the price of the key ingredient in her pies falls, Marilyn's expenses will fall and her profits will rise, assuming the number of pies that she sells remains unchanged.

Example 26
○ *Kinds of investments include ownership of businesses, debt, and commodities.*
○ *Commodities are tangible goods that people buy and sell as investments.*

Forms of ownership of businesses include:
• complete ownership of sole proprietorships
• partial ownership of partnerships
• shares of stock

Kinds of certificates of debt include:
• bills
• notes
• bonds

Kinds of commodities include:
• metals (such as gold, silver, or copper)
• grains (such as wheat, corn, or barley)
• sources of energy (such as crude oil or natural gas)
• sources of meat (such as cattle or hogs)
• materials for fabric (such as cotton or wool)
• works of art
• bottles of wine

Example 27

○ *People invest money to accumulate more money.*

○ *Levels of demand and supply determine values at which prices of investments reach equilibrium in the same way that they determine such values for goods.*

○ *The nominal return on a unit of an investment that its holder will have earned over a period of time will equal the quotient of his total gain from it over the period and its price at the beginning of the period, expressed as a percentage.*

Suppose the owners of a company decide to borrow money by selling thirty thousand bonds that obligate the company to pay $1000 per bond to their bearers two years after the date of issue. At the time the company sells the bonds, the supply of the bonds will equal 30,000 at every price. The demand for the bonds at higher prices will be less than the demand for the bonds at lower prices on the interval from $0 to $1000; however, the demand for the bonds will equal zero at all prices above $1000 because such prices would not allow the buyers of the bonds to earn positive returns on their investments.

Figure 17 shows the graphs of supply and demand for these particular bonds. Observe that the graphs intersect at

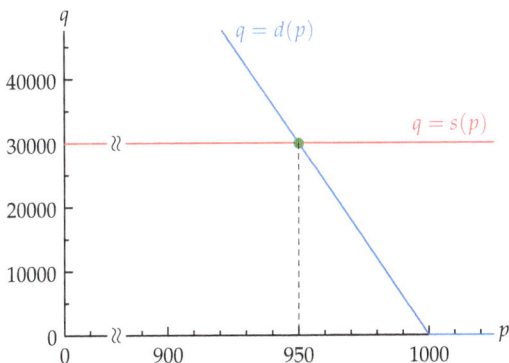

Figure 17: Graphs of Supply and Demand for Bonds

the point $(950, 30000)$, indicating that the price of the bonds will reach equilibrium at \$950. At this price, the owners of the company will maximize the amount they can borrow in the sale of the bonds.

If indeed the owners sell the bonds at a price of \$950, then the total gain to their buyers on each bond after two years will be \$50. Hence the nominal return that the buyers will have earned on their investment over the period of two years is 5.26% (see Formula 9).

$$\begin{aligned} \text{return on investment} &= (\$1000 - \$950)/\$950 \\ &= 0.0526 \\ &= 5.26\% \end{aligned}$$

Formula 9: Return on Investment

Example 28

○ *The annual yield on a unit of an investment is the quotient of the annual income paid to him who holds it and the current price at which he can sell it in the market.*

○ *The yield on an investment will fall when its price rises and rise when its price falls.*

Suppose that Table 4 shows the five highest bid prices, the five lowest ask prices, and the bid and ask sizes at those prices of limit orders for shares of stock in company Y that remain unfilled. We can use this information to generate the graphs of supply and demand shown in Figure 18. Ob-

Bid	Size		Ask	Size
14.28	200		14.34	200
14.29	900		14.35	600
14.30	100		14.36	400
14.31	700		14.37	500
14.32	300		14.38	800

Table 4: Bid and Ask Prices and Sizes for Shares in Y

serve that no more shares will be exchanged until someone offers to buy shares at higher prices or sell shares at lower prices.

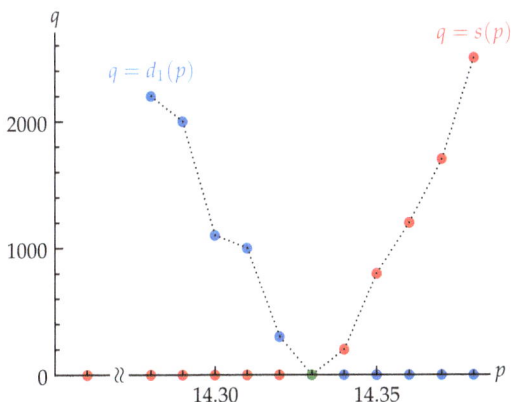

Figure 18: Graphs of Supply and Demand for Shares in Y
before Market Order

If we assume that the last price at which investors exchanged such shares was $14.33 and that the annual dividend per share of the stock is $0.79, then the current yield on the shares is 5.51% (see Formula 10).

$$
\begin{aligned}
\text{annual yield} &= \$0.79/\$14.33 \\
&= 0.0551 \\
&= 5.51\%
\end{aligned}
$$

Formula 10: Yield before Market Order

Now suppose an investor places a market order to buy 1200 shares of the stock and market makers execute the trade at $14.36 (the value at which the price would now reach equilibrium; see Figure 19). Then the price of the stock will have risen by $0.03 and the current yield will have fallen to 5.50% (see Formula 11).

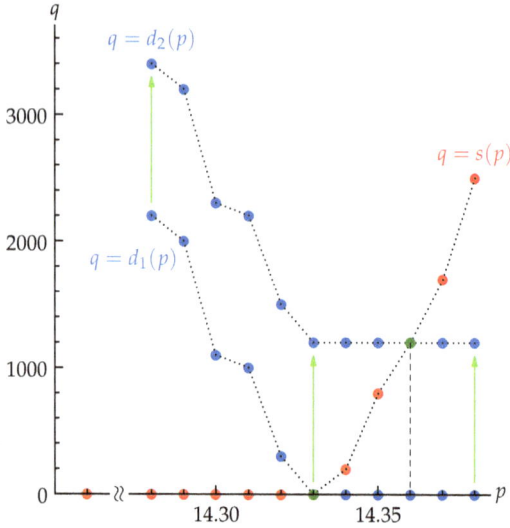

Figure 19: Graphs of Supply and Demand for Shares in Y
after Market Order

$$\text{annual yield} = \$0.79 / \$14.36$$
$$= 0.0550$$
$$= 5.50\%$$

Formula 11: Yield after Market Order

Example 29

○ *The real return to an investor on a unit of an investment over a period of time with respect to a good will equal the quotient of his total gain from the unit over the period in terms of the good and the quantity of the good that he could have bought with the proceeds from the sale of the unit at the beginning of the period, expressed as a percentage.*

○ *On an investment with no yield, an investor will earn a positive nominal return but suffer a negative real return with respect to a good if the percentage by which the price of the investment has risen is less than the percentage by which the price of the good has risen.*

Horace can purchase 25 chickens for $4 apiece on June 1. Instead of buying the chickens, he decides to invest $100 in shares of stock of company Z in the hope of buying more chickens at a later time with his proceeds from the sale of the shares.

Three months later on September 1, the value of his shares in Z have risen to $110. Horace sells them quickly, thereby earning a nominal profit of $10 and a nominal return of 10% on his investment (see Formula 12); however, the price of chickens has also risen and they now sell for $5 apiece. Horace can now purchase only 22 chickens. He has suffered a real loss of 3 chickens on his investment and earned a real return of -12% with respect to chickens (see Formula 13).

$$\text{nominal return} = (\$110 - \$100)/\$100$$
$$= 0.10$$
$$= 10\%$$

Formula 12: Nominal Return

$$\text{real return} = ((\$110/\$5) - (\$100/\$4))/(\$100/\$4)$$
$$= (22 - 25)/25$$
$$= -0.12$$
$$= -12\%$$

Formula 13: Real Return with Respect to Chickens

Example 30
The capitalization of a business is the product of the current price per share of ownership in the business and the total number of such shares outstanding.

Suppose that directors of corporation B have issued a total of 80 million shares of its stock and that the current price of each share is $7.15. Then the capitalization of corporation B is $572 million (equal to 80 million × $7.15).

The capitalization of corporation B will change by $80 million for every increase or decrease of $1 in the price of the shares. Hence if the price of the shares rises to $8.15, then the capitalization will rise to $652 million.

Example 31

○ *The profit of a producer will fall when the demand for his good falls, the prices of the ingredients, labor, and plant that he uses rise, or his operation becomes less efficient.*

○ *Decreases in profit will tend to lead to lower rates of production and levels of supply of the good.*

Suppose that manufacturers M_1, M_2, M_3, and M_4 produce identical frying pans of iron at the levels of expense, revenue, and profit indicated in Table 5 (monetary amounts in pounds of copper). We will treat all pans as units of the same good under the assumptions that all manufacturers sell their pans from the same location, offer the same levels of service to their customers, provide the same warranties on their products, etc.

Maker	Expense Per Pan	Revenue Per Pan	Profit Per Pan	Daily Production	Daily Profit
M_1	6.20	8.70	2.50	50	125
M_2	6.70	8.70	2.00	50	100
M_3	7.20	8.70	1.50	50	75
M_4	7.70	8.70	1.00	50	50

Table 5: Profits on Pans

Some time later, an increase in the cost of iron causes the expense of each manufacturer to rise by 1.20 pounds per pan. We revise our calculations of profit as indicated in Table 6.

M_4 now loses money in the production of frying pans and decides to stop making them, causing the total daily production of pans to fall from 200 to 150 and the value at

Maker	Expense Per Pan	Revenue Per Pan	Profit Per Pan	Daily Production	Daily Profit
M_1	7.40	8.70	1.30	50	65
M_2	7.90	8.70	0.80	50	40
M_3	8.40	8.70	0.30	50	15
M_4	8.90	8.70	−0.20	50	−10

Table 6: Profits on Pans after Increase in Expense

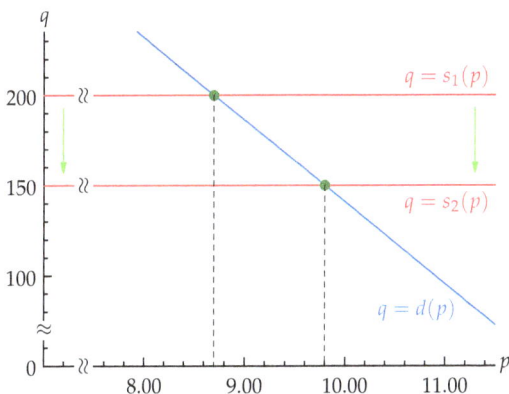

Figure 20: Graphs of Supply and Demand for Pans

which the price of the pans reaches equilibrium to rise to 9.80 pounds (see Figure 20).

Each of the three remaining manufacturers M_1, M_2, and M_3 quickly raises the price of his pans to \$9.80. We revise our calculations of profit again as indicated in Table 7. Observe that the daily profit for each of the three manufacturers now lies only slightly below its original level.

Maker	Expense Per Pan	Revenue Per Pan	Profit Per Pan	Daily Production	Daily Profit
M_1	7.40	9.80	2.40	50	120
M_2	7.90	9.80	1.90	50	95
M_3	8.40	9.80	1.40	50	70

Table 7: Profits on Pans after Increase in Revenue

Example 32
A producer cannot assure himself of greater revenue and profit by simply raising the price of his good because the demand for the good at the higher price will be less than the demand for the good at the current price.

Karl produces and sells 7,000 jars of strawberry jam each month at a profit of $5 per jar. One year, a blight causes the production of strawberries to fall and the price of strawberries to rise. As a result, the cost of production of the jam rises by $2 per jar.

To preserve his profits, Karl decides to raise the price of his jam by $2 per jar; however, he can sell only 500 jars each month at the higher price. At this level of sales, Karl cannot cover the fixed costs of his business and begins to suffer substantial losses on his operations. Six months after his decision to raise the price of his product, Karl files for bankruptcy and returns to the slums.

Example 33
As people fill the earth, they will discover areas of the world in which they can extract minerals, grow crops, or raise livestock of new kinds or in higher quantities.

Through exploration, people found:
- pineapple on tropical islands
- whales in the oceans from which to extract oil
- fertile land in the Ukraine on which to grow wheat
- gold in Peru

Example 34
To satisfy their physical needs and wants more adequately, people seek to consume goods of higher quality and in greater quantities.

A. Peter has a bicycle, but he would like to have a car.

B. Otis has a small car, but he would like to have a large car.

C. Helena has a large car, but she would like to have two large cars.

D. Kermit has two large cars, but he would also like to have a pickup truck with big wheels.

E. Robert can afford to eat one cookie each day, but he would like to eat a dozen cookies each day.

Example 35
The price of a good at equilibrium measures the need of partici-pants in the market for greater production of that good in com-parison to other goods.

Producer C produces lanterns at a cost of $50 apiece and sells them for $100 apiece. Producer D produces similar lanterns at a cost of $50 but can sell them for only $80. The need of the members of society for more lanterns of C is greater than their need for more lanterns of D.

Example 36
○ *A profit on operations indicates that a producer has transformed goods that the members of society need less into goods that they need more.*
○ *A loss on operations indicates that a producer has destructively transformed goods that the members of society need more into goods that they need less.*

A mechanic can build a fancy car and sell it at the high price of £200,000; however, his expense to build it would be £225,000. The high price of the car indicates that the members of society have great need for its production. But the higher cost of its manufacture indicates that they have even greater need for the ingredients, labor, and plant used therein. Since those goods would meet greater needs with-out the manufacture of the car than within it, the mechanic should not build the car.

Example 37
○ *Two kinds of money exist: real and substitutive.*
○ *Real money is a physical commodity.*
○ *Different commodities have served as monetary material at different places and times in history.*

Historical monetary material includes:
• salt, sugar, and shells
• pelts, cattle, and tobacco
• paper
• gold, silver, and copper

Example 38
Substitutive money is a direct claim on real money.

Kinds of substitutive money include:
• notes
• entries in ledgers at banks

Means of transferring substitutive money include:
• passing a note
• writing a cheque
• sending a wire

Example 39
○ *The prospect of greater wealth can tempt a banker to lend real money on which he has issued substitutive money.*
○ *Bankers can produce substitutive money in a quantity that far exceeds the quantity of the real money that undergirds it.*
○ *Substitutive money divides into two classes: realizable and unrealizable.*

Suppose person P_1 deposits five coins in a bank. Managers at the bank credit the account of P_1 for five coins, but then lend the coins to person P_2, who trades them to person P_3 for some good. At this point P_3 holds the five coins, but P_1 also believes that he owns five coins and will conduct his affairs under this presumption. Thus P_1 and P_3 together claim ownership of ten coins, of which only five really exist. Hence there exist five units of real money and five units of unrealizable substitutive money.

Further suppose that P_3 now deposits the five coins in the bank, its managers then lend them to person P_4, and P_4 then trades them to person P_5. At this point P_5 holds the five coins, but P_1 and P_3 also each believe that they own five coins. There now exist five units of real money and ten units of unrealizable substitutive money.

Example 40

○ *No banker can immediately redeem claims on real money that he does not hold.*
○ *A default on debt may leave the owner of a bank unable to discharge his own liabilities to depositors.*

Suppose a banker retains in reserve 20% of every deposit placed in his bank. Consider the transactions below.

1. Seller S_0 deposits 625 grams of gold in the bank.
2. The bank retains 125 grams of the deposit of S_0 and lends 500 grams to borrower B_1.
3. B_1 spends the 500 grams on goods of seller S_1, who deposits the money in the bank.
4. The bank retains 100 grams of the deposit of S_1 and lends 400 grams to borrower B_2.
5. B_2 spends the 400 grams on goods of seller S_2, who deposits the money in the bank.
6. The bank retains 80 grams of the deposit of S_2 and lends 320 grams to borrower B_3.
7. B_3 spends the 320 grams on goods of seller S_3, who deposits the money in the bank.
8. The bank retains 64 grams of the deposit of S_3 and lends 256 grams to borrower B_4.
9. B_4 spends the 256 grams on goods of seller S_4, who deposits the money in the bank.

The banker records these transactions in a ledger with the entries shown in Table 8. Observe that after S_4 makes his deposit:

- the banker will hold 625 grams of gold
- borrowers will owe the banker 1476 grams of gold
- the banker will owe depositors 2101 grams of gold

Assets

	Gold				Loans	
	Debit	Credit			Debit	Credit
1	625			2	500	
2		500		4	400	
3	500			6	320	
4		400		8	256	
5	400					
6		320			1476	
7	320					
8		256				
9	256					
	2101	1476				

Liabilities

	Deposits	
	Debit	Credit
1		625
3		500
5		400
7		320
9		256
		2101

Table 8: Ledger of Bank

The banker has generated 2101 grams of substitutive gold on the initial deposit of S_0 of 625 grams of real gold.

Of these 2101 grams, 625 are realizable and 1476 are un-realizable. Thus the banker would not be able to redeem immediately all the claims of the depositors to their gold.

In general, a banker who retains in reserve $r\%$ of all deposits placed in his bank can generate $d/r\%$ units of substitutive money on an initial deposit of d units of real money. Of this substitutive money, only d units will be realizable. Hence if we extended this example to an infinite number of transactions made in the same pattern, then ultimately the banker would have generated 3125 grams of substitutive gold from the initial deposit of S_0 of 625 grams. Of these 3125 grams, 625 would be realizable and 2500 would be unrealizable.

14

Examples for Part II

Example 41
○ *We will define the term controller to mean anyone who uses force, whether directly or through subordinates, to take full or partial control of the person or property of someone else.*
○ *A controller may operate in service to an organization or on his own behalf.*

Kinds of controllers who often work alone include:
• vandals
• arsonists
• thieves
• kidnappers
• murderers

Kinds of controllers who usually work within an organization include:
• kingpins of criminal syndicates
• members of violent urban gangs
• jailers
• executioners
• police officers and soldiers
• bureaucrats
• publicans
• judges
• mayors, commissioners, governors, presidents, and kings
• wealthy men who control nominal heads of state
• women who control men who control heads of state

Example 42

○ *A controller can steal property from people.*
○ *Controllers in government steal regularly and systematically in the name of taxation.*
○ *A tax on the sale of a good harms its seller.*

Every month a dealer buys 27 cars of a particular model and sells them at a price of 61.00 pounds of silver per car. Suddenly and capriciously, the queen imposes a tax of 8% on all revenues that dealers earn on retail sales of cars. The tax will not alter the schedule of demand for the cars of the dealer, so the value at which their price to buyers reaches equilibrium will remain at 61.00 pounds. But if the dealer fails to lower the price he lists on the cars, then their cost to buyers will rise to 65.88 (or 61.00 × 1.08) pounds. At this cost, he will sell only 22 cars per month (see Figure 21).

To sell all the 27 cars that he bought in the month after the tax was imposed and avoid a surplus, the dealer must reduce their listed price to 56.48 (or 61.00 ÷ 1.08) pounds; the sum of the listed price and the tax will then equate to 61.00 pounds. Thus the tax will reduce the monthly revenue of the dealer by 4.52 pounds per car and 122.04 pounds in total. The customers will pay the same amount of money

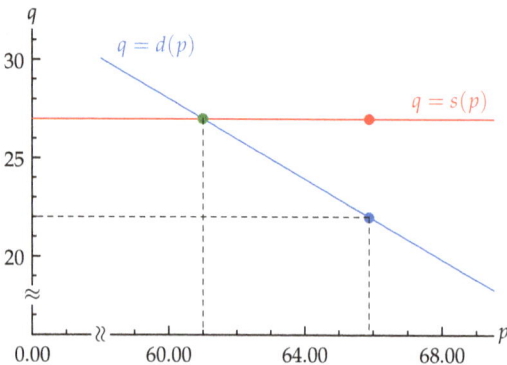

Figure 21: Graphs of Supply and Demand for Cars

for the cars as before.

In the future, the dealer likely will not try to sell 27 cars per month, especially if he loses money by doing so. He may even stop selling cars altogether. But any reduction in the number of cars that he offers for sale will cause their price to reach equilibrium at a higher value. In the long run then, the tax will also affect adversely potential buyers of the cars because it will either prevent them from buying one or force them to pay more money for it.

Note that if the sales of the dealer were indeed to fall, then the amount of money that the royal treasury would receive from the tax will be less than the amount of money that the queen might have expected at the time she imposed it. A tax sufficiently high to completely extinguish sales of cars would provide no financial gain to her Majesty.

Example 43
Employees, not employers, bear the cost of all taxes on wages.

Susie earns £9.20 per hour by washing dishes at a particular restaurant. Its owner cannot afford to pay more for her services. Suddenly, legislators impose a tax of 10% on the earnings of employees and a tax of 15% on the payroll of employers. These taxes will not alter the schedule of demand of the owner for the labor of Susie; he will remain willing to pay £9.20 per hour at maximum for her services. But he would now pay £1.20 to the government and £8.00 to Susie, who would then pay £0.80 to the government and retain £7.20 in net earnings. Thus Susie would bear the entire cost of both taxes of £2.00 per hour.

Susie may decide not to work at the restaurant at this lower rate of compensation; however, the taxes will diminish wages she might earn elsewhere to the same degree as those at her job in the restaurant. If she could not earn a wage higher than £9.20 per hour before the imposition of the tax, then she will not likely earn a net wage higher than £7.20 per hour now.

Example 44

○ *A ceiling is an arbitrary upper limit on the price at which a controller allows a person to sell units of a good.*

○ *A shortage of a good will exist at the maximum price established by an effective ceiling.*

○ *An effective ceiling will harm the seller of the good affected.*

Tom produces 750 bolts per day at a cost of $0.53 per bolt. He sells the bolts for $0.73 apiece, which is the value at which their price has reached equilibrium (see Figure 22). Thus Tom earns a profit of $0.20 per bolt.

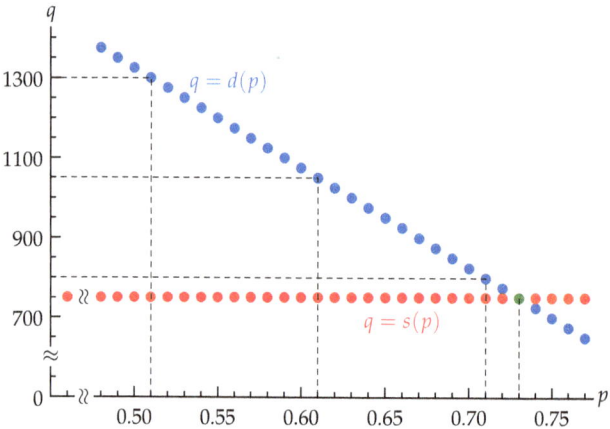

Figure 22: Graphs of Supply and Demand for Bolts

Suppose now that a controller plans to impose a ceiling on the price of Tom's bolts. Let us consider the effects of ceilings of $0.81, $0.71, $0.61, and $0.51.

- A ceiling of $0.81 will have no effect on Tom or his customers because it would lie above the price of the bolts at equilibrium.
- At a price of $0.71, customers will seek to buy 800 bolts. Thus a ceiling of $0.71 will reduce Tom's profit to $0.18 per

138

bolt and lead immediately to a daily shortage of 50 bolts.
- At a price of \$0.61, customers will seek to buy 1050 bolts. Thus a ceiling of \$0.61 will reduce Tom's profit to \$0.08 per bolt and lead to a daily shortage of 300 bolts.
- At a price of \$0.51, customers will seek to buy 1300 bolts. Thus a ceiling of \$0.51 will cause Tom to suffer a loss of \$0.02 per bolt and lead to a daily shortage of 550 bolts.

The calculations above assume that Tom will continue to produce bolts at a rate of 750 per day; however, he may well reduce his rate of production at a ceiling of \$0.71 or \$0.61 and will likely discontinue production altogether at a ceiling of \$0.51. Reduction of production would exacerbate any shortage.

Example 45
○ *A floor is an arbitrary lower limit on the price at which a controller allows a producer to sell units of a good.*
○ *A surplus of a good will exist at the minimum price established by an effective floor.*
○ *An effective floor will harm all potential buyers of the good affected.*
○ *A minimum wage is a floor on the price of labor.*

Ursula earns £8.00 per hour by washing dishes at a restaurant but would like to earn more money for no extra labor. She decides to agitate before members of the legislature and successfully petitions them to establish a minimum wage of £10.00 per hour.

Ursula rejoices; however, the owner of restaurant cannot afford to pay either her or his other employees (including her friend Susie; see Example 43) more than £8.00 per hour. He subsequently relieves all his employees of their duties and closes the restaurant. Ursula now cannot find another job and blames capitalism for her lack of opportunities. In her ignorance of economics, she does not blame herself or the legislators.

Example 46

○ *A controller can prohibit a producer from selling a good in quantities above some upper limit.*

○ *A restriction on sales will harm all potential buyers of the good.*

○ *A restriction on sales will harm the potential seller of the good.*

○ *Only a controller can grant and enforce a privilege of monopoly over all goods of a certain kind.*

○ *A privilege of monopoly granted to a producer will eliminate the supply of the goods of his competitors and raise the demand for his own good.*

○ *A privilege of monopoly can take the form of a license, patent, or copyright.*

A. Suppose inspectors prohibit merchants from importing carpets from Persia. Then buyers of carpets will not be able to obtain them from Persia and will pay more money for carpets from other sources. Thus the profits of Persian makers of carpets will fall while the profits of non-Persian makers of carpets will rise.

B. Suppose municipal authorities limit the number of drivers who can transport passengers to and from the airport by taxi. Then passengers will pay more money for this service to the drivers given license to provide it, but willing drivers not allowed to provide it must take less profitable routes.

C. Suppose legislators grant copyright to the author of a book and prohibit publishers from producing copies of the book without his permission. Then readers will pay more money and the author will earn more money in the sale of copies of the book; however, publishers who would like to print and sell them but cannot obtain permission to do so must print less lucrative literature.

Example 47

○ *A controller can compel a person to expend labor and resources to produce a good in greater quantities.*

○ *Compulsion of production will help buyers of the good.*
○ *Compulsion of production will harm the slave.*

A. Suppose a king enslaves members of a particular tribe and forces them to pick cotton for him. Then buyers will pay less money for cotton and the king will earn money on its sale, but the slaves will see no benefit from their labor.

B. Suppose National Socialists force the owners of a factory to produce poison gas for the state instead of fertilizer for farmers. Then farmers will pay more money for fertilizer from other sources and the owners of the factory will earn a lower profit, but other producers of fertilizer will earn higher profits and the state will have poison gas.

Example 48
○ *A controller can compel people to purchase a good.*
○ *Compulsion of consumption will help the seller of the good.*
○ *Compulsion of consumption will harm buyers of the good.*

A. Suppose governmental authorities force parents to vaccinate their children against a certain disease. Then the price of the vaccine and the profits of the pharmaceutical companies that produce it will rise, but parents who would not have purchased the vaccine for their children will have less money to spend on other goods.

B. Suppose the commissioner of insurance forces the residents of his state to buy insurance against unexpected medical expenses. Then insurers will earn higher profits, but people who were not insured before the mandate will have less money to spend on other goods.

C. Suppose a controller prevents an employer from terminating workers that he does not need. Then the employer must continue to pay money for useless labor, but the workers will continue to hold jobs.

Example 49

○ *A controller can prohibit consumers from purchasing a good in quantities above some upper limit.*

○ *A restriction on consumption will harm the seller of the good.*

○ *A restriction on consumption will harm people who cannot now buy the good in the quantities they desire.*

A. Suppose authorities prohibit all people under 30 years old from purchasing cigarettes. Then older smokers will pay less money for a pack of cigarettes, but younger smokers will be less able to satisfy their addictions to nicotine and the profits of manufacturers of cigarettes will fall.

B. Suppose members of the council of a city prohibit yellow people from riding on buses within the city. Then people who are not yellow will pay less money for fares on buses, but yellow people will be deprived of a means of transportation and the profits of operators of buses will fall.

Example 50

○ *A controller can force producers to follow certain rules in order to sell their goods.*

○ *A regulation on sales will usually harm producers.*

A. Suppose the mayor of a certain town issues a decree that all restaurants within the limits of the town must provide washrooms for their customers to use. One restaurant in the town does not have a washroom. Through his decree, the mayor imposes on the owner of this restaurant not only a cost to build and equip a washroom, but also recurring costs for water, towels, cleansers, access to the sewer, janitorial services, and so forth. Thus the mayor will add to the expenses of the owner and reduce his profit.

B. Suppose bureaucrats force prospective doctors to attend school for many years and to pass rigorous examinations before they allow them to practice medicine. As the supply of medical services falls, patients will pay more money for them and the wages of doctors allowed to practice medicine will rise. But compassionate people who would like to help heal the sick but cannot satisfy the conditions of the bureaucrats must pursue less rewarding opportunities.

Example 51

○ *Standards of quality on goods do not fail to exist in the absence of an idealistic controller.*

○ *Goods can become less durable, less reliable, or more hazardous after controllers enact standards for these qualities.*

A. In a free market, owners will keep their restaurants sanitary because they will lose business if they serve food that makes their customers sick.

B. In a free market, people will conduct research on the safety, durability, and reliability of goods because consumers will pay them for this information.

C. In a free market, officers of companies will hire accountants to audit their books in order to attract money from new investors and to placate current investors. The accountants that they hire will examine the books closely because they will lose credibility and clients if they fail to discover errors in financial records or to warn of impending insolvency.

D. If a regulators claim to oversee the activities of a banker, then many depositors will assume that his bank is sound and will not bother to seek and analyze its financial statements.

E. If an official in the government issues a license to a doctor to practice medicine, then many patients will assume his competence, accept his plans of treatment without question, and fail to probe his background for cases of fraudulence or misdiagnosis.

Example 52

○ *If a controller enables people to avoid productive activity, then he will reduce production.*

○ *Less production will necessitate less consumption.*

Suppose ten men live on an island. They produce and consume 5 fish per day apiece and 50 fish per day in total. If one of the men dies, then the total number of fish they produce will decline to 45, but the average number of fish they produce will remain at 5. But if one of the men assumes an unproductive bureaucratic position on the island, then the total number of fish they produce will decline to 45 and the average number of fish they produce will decline to 4.5. The level of consumption per capita will then have fallen by the percentage (namely 10%) of the men who have become idle and unproductive.

Example 53

○ *A controller may disburse a portion of his plunder to sellers or buyers of goods in the form of subsidies.*

○ *When given to the seller himself, a subsidy will cause his profit to rise directly by the amount of the subsidy.*

○ *A subsidy will cause levels of supply of a good to rise eventually and its price to reach equilibrium at a lower value.*

○ *The total cost of a subsidy may rise beyond the initial estimates of a controller.*

The farmers of a county produce 490 thousand bushels of wheat per year and earn a profit of 0.60 grams of silver per bushel on revenues of 3.25 grams per bushel and expenses of 2.65 grams per bushel.

In the year of an election, the unpopular commissioner of the county decides to grant these farmers a permanent subsidy on production of wheat of 0.80 grams per bushel. This subsidy raises their revenues to 4.05 grams per bushel and profit to 1.40 grams per bushel. But the high profits now motivate farmers who had been growing corn to grow wheat. The following year, the total production of wheat expands to 670 thousand bushels per year and the price of wheat at equilibrium drops to 2.45 grams per bushel (see Figure 23). Thus the profit that the farmers earn on wheat has returned to 0.60 grams per bushel.

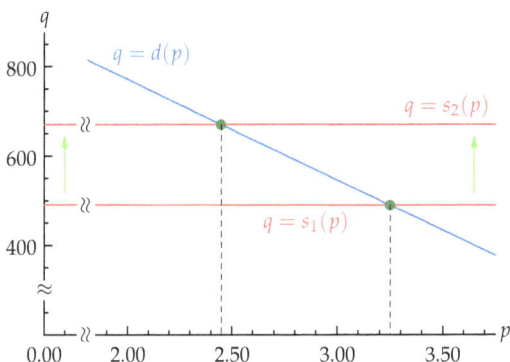

Figure 23: Graphs of Supply and Demand Curves for Wheat

The actions of the commissioner initially brought higher profits to the growers of wheat, but now they earn profits no higher than they did before the implementation of the subsidy. Yet those actions have caused the annual production of wheat in the county to rise by 180 thousand bushels. Hence the commissioner has burdened the county (or rather, the payers of his taxes) with an annual expenditure of 536 thousand grams instead of the 392 thousand grams that he had originally expected. If he now decides to eliminate the subsidy, the farmers will suffer a loss of 0.20 grams on every bushel of wheat they produce until the total production thereof falls back to its original level.

Example 54
When given to buyers of the good, a subsidy will cause the profit of the seller to rise indirectly as it causes levels of demand for the

good to rise and its price to reach equilibrium at a higher value.

At a price of $500, 250 students will enroll in a particular class. Suppose now that the Minister of Education decides to grant a subsidy of $200 to everyone who enrolls in the class. Since every prospective student now can afford to pay $200 more to take the class than he could before, the number of students who now seek to take it at any given price p will equal the number who previously sought to take it at the price $p - $200. Thus the graph of demand for a seat in the classroom will shift to the right by $200 (see Figure 24).

Although more students would now like to enroll in the class at the price of $500, the classroom will hold only 250 seats. Thus the value at which the price of a seat in the classroom reaches equilibrium will rise to $700. At this price, the professor will now earn a total of $175,000 for his work instead of $125,000. Hence the subsidy has helped the seller of the service, but it has not helped the buyers at all.

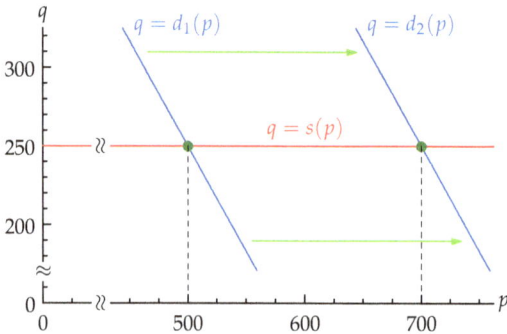

Figure 24: Graphs of Supply and Demand for Seats

About the Author

The author was born in North Dakota and resides presently in Oregon.

www.ingramcontent.com/pod-product-compliance
Lightning Source LLC
Chambersburg PA
CBHW050728030426
42336CB00012B/1466